The Music of
PAUL BEN-HAIM

a performance guide

by

HADASSAH GUTTMANN

The Scarecrow Press, Inc.
Metuchen, N.J., & London
1992

This book is based on the author's dissertation, "Selected Instrumental Works of Paul Ben-Haim: a Performance Guide," New York University, 1991.

British Library Cataloguing-in-Publication data available

Library of Congress Cataloging-in-Publication Data

Guttmann, Hadassah, 1952-
    The music of Paul Ben-Haim : a performance guide / by Hadassah Guttmann.
    p.   cm.
    "List of Ben-Haim's works" : p.
    Discography: p.
    ISBN 0-8108-2551-1 (acid-free paper)
    1. Ben-Haim, Paul. 1897- Instrumental music. 2. Instrumental music—Analysis, appreciation. I. Title.
ML410.B44909 1992   92-5279
784 .092—dc20

Copyright © 1992 by Hadassah Guttmann
Manufactured in the United States of America
Printed on acid-free paper

I dedicate this work to the loving memory of my mother,
Helen Guttmann

ACKNOWLEDGMENTS

I wish to thank my friend and colleague, Professor Russell Bliss for his invaluable technical help in producing this book. His unfailing optimism and generous moral support made the task much less arduous than it could have been.

My thanks also to Mrs. Masha Benya Matz for her help in translating several documents from the Hebrew originals.

It is with gratitude and affection that I thank Mrs. Hely Ben-Haim for her help and her kind words of encouragement.

And to Paul Ben-Haim himself for his words of praise when I had the privilege of performing several of his works for him.

Dr. Hadassah Guttmann
Nassau Community College,
Garden City, New York
and Lucy Moses School,
New York City

Contents

Acknowledgments	v
Introduction	1
Chapter 1 Ben-Haim and the Music of Israel	11
Chapter 2 Sonatina	21
Timeline	35
Chapter 3 Five Pieces for Piano	39
Timeline	62
Chapter 4 Melody and Variations	66
Timeline	73
Chapter 5 Three Songs Without Words	75
Timeline	91
Chapter 6 Variations on a Hebrew Melody	94
Timeline	123
Chapter 7 Quintet for Clarinet and String Quartet	128
Timeline	149
Chapter 8 Sonata in G for Violin Solo	156
Timeline	171
Chapter 9 Serenade	174
Timeline	188
Chapter 10 Improvisation and Dance	192
Timeline	197
Chapter 11 Arabic Song	199
Timeline	204
Chapter 12 Performance Guide	205

Chapter 13 Summary and Conclusions   236

Bibliography   240

Appendixes

    A List of Ben-Haim's Works   244
    B Discography   246
    C Letters Reflecting Ben-Haim's Stature   249

Index   253

About the Author   255

Introduction

The focus for this study is to investigate several selected instrumental works of Paul Ben-Haim; to identify their place in modern instrumental literature and provide a performance guide for the selected compositions. The author also surveyed the background and musical training of Paul Ben-Haim and presented an overview of his instrumental works.

The selected works were analyzed to determine the structural elements of these compositions and to reveal the composer's style. Allied with this was an examination of interpretive problems of performance existent in the pieces and to develop suggestions for performance based on those findings.

The first step was to survey the background and musical training of Paul Ben-Haim, and to present an overview of his chamber and piano works. Second, the selected works were analyzed for their structural elements, and third, the interpretive problems of performance in the selected works were examined to understand the composer's style.

The fourth step was to develop a performance guide based on previous findings.

Paul Ben-Haim is considered to be one of Israel's foremost composers.[1] Among the older group of European-trained musicians he is the best known. He is regarded as "... the earliest and foremost creator of musical style, the melismatic melodies, the intricate rhythms and the characteristic colouring of which had come to reflect the very special atmosphere of the land of Israel..."[2] However, for a musician of his stature his works have suffered from unjustified neglect in recent years (1991). They deserve to be heard, and would be a valuable addition to a performer's repertoire.

A testament to his stature is made evident by the fact that such renowned artists as Leonard Bernstein, Leopold Stokowski and Jascha Heifetz have performed his works and thought highly of them (see Appendix C.)

Ben-Haim, as a teacher and mentor, has had a considerable impact on many Israeli composers, both of his generation and of later generations. He was the recipient of the Israeli State Prize, the Tel Aviv Municipality's "Yoel Engel Prize," and many other awards.[3]

Although many of his works are known and have been performed internationally, his music has been largely ignored recently in the areas of performance, research and criticism. The author has had great difficulty in obtaining scores of some of Ben-Haim's compositions, such as the String Quartet and the Piano Quartet. It is clear that this composer's music has been neglected without justification. It is hoped that this research will stimulate interest in and enthusiasm for Paul Ben-Haim's chamber and piano works, and help resurrect them from their long and undeserved obscurity. However, it should be noted that in Israel, Ben-Haim is far from forgotten, as his music is heard on the radio more than any other Israeli composer. Also live performances of his works have been flourishing there for some time, and in addition, there is a Ben-Haim Competition for young musicians who play Israeli music.

Since an extensive analysis of every work of Paul Ben-Haim was too long for this study, a process of selection was used to choose a portion of the works from his total corpus. The goal was to select a manageable number of pieces which were representative of a cross section of the East-West synthesis found in the composer's output. After extensive research the writer chose the chamber and piano works as being the most frequently cited in the literature and representative of the composer's style. Peter Gradenwitz writes: "The chamber and piano music are the composer's best medium of expression."[4] James Friskin and Irwin Freundlich, two distinguished pedagogues both believed that Ben-Haim's piano music was "... a unique contribution to the modern keyboard repertoire."[5]

The proportional incidence of chamber works in relation to the total number of solo piano compositions gives a ratio of two to one. As earlier works were considered derivative,[6] this author has chosen ten later pieces written after 1936 because of their frequency of citation in the literature; three pieces for piano solo and six chamber works keep the two to one ratio. Two of the shorter chamber works, *Arabic Song* and *Improvisation and Dance*, have been treated as one.

Innovative ideas, not necessarily Middle-Eastern influenced, including rhythmic patterns, harmonic development, and structural growth were taken into consideration during the selection process.

The degree of possibility for a credible performance of the work was evaluated. The availability of musical scores, instruments and other technical, financial, and esthetic demands of the piece was taken into account. The more accessible, the greater the weight that was assigned to the work. The goal was to select a manageable number of pieces which were representative of the East-West synthesis found in his works. The primary sources were the music itself and the data generated from the modified La Rue analysis and the timelines.

La Rue Analysis

La Rue analysis is considered to be an objective system of analyzing the structural and stylistic elements inherent in any given work. The timelines, derived from this analysis, represent a visual illustration of these elements, and provide a working model of musical events as they happen.

The La Rue analysis is broken down into three categories. The stylistic analysis consists of an examination of each composition's content which includes sound, harmony, rhythm and melody. The structural analysis investigates the architectural design, which consists of clarity, proportion, integrity, complexity and subtlety. Finally, timelines were created to graphically represent how the music unfolds.

The performance guide was developed based on an analysis of the stylistic and structural elements endemic to the music. The primary sources were the musical scores and the data generated therein.

The method of style analysis used in this study is based on a system created by Jan La Rue and set forth in his book.[7] La Rue employs the fundamental materials of music: sound, harmony, melody and form. In a revised form fashioned by Walter Reinhold, the analysis was divided into the "Stylistic Level," and the "Structural Level." First the music was analyzed within the separate headings: Sonority, Harmony, Rhythm and Melody. Second, the music was analyzed in relation to its Clarity, Proportion, Integrity, Complexity and Subtlety. Following this, La Rue's "Timeline" concept was used. This produces a linear model that graphically portrays the outstanding features and proportions of the work in question.

Stylistic Level

Sonority

The dynamic range of intensity and dynamic types and their frequency of appearance is discussed. The range and texture of the sound is taken into account. Any special effects and sudden dynamic changes are noted. Climaxes receive special attention since they often dictate or draw attention to significant structural areas. The degree of contrasts and timbre is explored with attention paid to range, registration, high points, low points and special effects. Any idiomatic usages helps to define the music's character. Finally, the density of the sound is examined through analysis of the textures.

Harmony

This embodies not only tonalities, but also any contrapuntal activity. Balances in harmonic textures are discussed, with attention to the complexities that are subsequently created. The chordal vocabulary is explored, especially for the treatment of dissonances, harmonic density, chordal progressions and resolutions. Bi-tonalities and areas of polytonality are highlighted. The harmonic relationships to climaxes also receive special attention.

Rhythm

Tempo indications are defined, and discussed for their meter's regularity or irregularity within each movement or section. General, overall rhythmic relationships with melody and harmony are explored as well as the relationship of rhythm to espressivity.

Melody

Melodic material is defined and discussed. Special charactaristics of each motif, such as range, phrase structure and lyric quality are noted. Melodic ideas are traced and their development followed throughout a movement or work.

Structural Level

Clarity

The category of Clarity includes a discussion of the distinctness of shape. Also addressed is the nature of the design of the music and its order, proportion and the nature of the articulations which define these parameters.

Proportion

This section deals with the clarity of the musical shapes and articulations. It determines whether the architecture is undergirded by balanced relationships within the entire work. The climaxes are of special note, since their impact is often a result of a logical and cohesive design.

Integrity

An assessment of the coherence and unity of the work or movement is explored in this category. Special attention is paid to the way transitions are handled. The smoothness or roughness of seams is noted. Concinnity, or the coordination of elements (sound, harmony, rhythm and melody) is scrutinized. In works containing more than one movement, these factors are observed within the movement and within the context of the whole piece.

Complexity

The degree and amount of contrasts is related to the unity of the work. Variety and balance of contrasting material is observed within each work, and between movements. The relationship between complexities and simplicities is related to tensions and releases. Finally, the presence of interesting detail, in single movement works and between movements, is observed.

Subtlety

The presence or absence of clichés is observed. The predictability of the music was discussed in two ways: first, how far it deviates from conventionality, and how much it satisfies our expectations.

The Timeline

Key to Symbols

A, B, C	Capital letters signify main theme groups.
Aab, Babc, etc	Lower-case letters represent a period within a theme area.
P, S	Primary and secondary themes. in sonata form.
x,y,z	Show phrases or sub-phrases. within a period.
T	Transition theme.
N	New theme or material.
I	Introductory material.

k	Closing material.
m.	Motive, thematic or rhythmic.
Pa^1, Pa^2	Superscript numbers denote slight variations such as altered registers or intervals.
V	A variation.

The format of the timeline

Tempo markings	*Allegro Molto Andante*, etc
Dynamic markings	*ff* *mf* *ppp*
Main sections	EXPOSITION
Motives, themes	A av^1 B Ba Bb
Measure numbers	1 2 7 9 12
Tonalities	D+ (D major) Cm (C minor)

Notes

1. Francis D. Perkins, *The New York Herald-Tribune*, April 25, 1959, p. 18
2. Peter Gradenwitz, *The Music of Israel*. (New York: Holt, Rinehart and Winston, Inc., 1954)
3. Gradenwitz, p.211
4. Gradenwitz, p. 272
5. James Friskin, Irwin Freundlich, *Music for Piano*. (New York: Holt, Rinehart and Winston, Inc., 1954)
6. Jehoash Hirshberg, *Paul Ben-Haim, His Life and Works*. (Tel Aviv: Am Oved Publishers, 1989)
7. Jan La Rue, *Guidelines for Style Analysis*. (New York: W.W. Norton & Company, Inc., 1970)

Chapter One

BEN-HAIM AND THE MUSIC OF ISRAEL

The cultural climate of Israel, like the USA, is largely influenced by the tension produced by different ethnic groups trying to live together. Israel is a land of immigrants with a common heritage, both national and historical.

The Israeli composer faces the same dilemma as composers all over the world—that of having his works performed and recorded. The size of Israel, with its limited number of symphony orchestras, chamber orchestras and string quartets is compounded by the fact that it is surrounded by Arab nations with which it has little, if any, contact or cultural exchange. The Israeli composer must turn to his own surroundings for sources.

Early Zionist settlers at the beginning of this century established music schools and instrumental ensembles that performed music of the classical and romantic repertory. The foundations for formal music education began to take shape in the 1930s. By the time the state was formed in 1948, there were already academies of music in Jerusalem and Tel Aviv, and a State Music Teachers Training College.

Among the large waves of immigrants in the 1930s were many highly skilled musicians who gave a strong impetus to Israel's musical life. The most important event of this embryonic culture was the founding in 1936 of the Israel Philharmonic Orchestra, then called the Palestine Symphony Orchestra, by the violinist Bronislaw Huberman (1882-1974).[1] Since its first concert under Arturo Toscanini in 1936, the orchestra has been the best known musical organization in the country. It has always included some works of local composers in its programs, and it is still the only outlet for those Israeli composers who write for large orchestra.

Israeli composers can be divided into two main groups. Those of the older generation came to Israel as adults with well-defined, professional musical backgrounds, acquired in their countries of origin, mainly Germany, Poland and Hungary. The younger composers were either born in Israel or came there at an early age and received their basic music education there. Many of them studied composition with the older group.

Most of the composers who came from Europe before World War II (like Ben-Haim) went through a period of adjustment to their new surroundings. They were affected by the rugged, ancient landscape with its spirit of the Bible, the rhythm of the Hebrew language, the idealization of a rural life that had been denied to Jews in the Diaspora and the Middle Eastern melos. During the 1930s and 40s many of them collected and arranged Eastern folk melodies, and sooner or later their works showed an influence of these activities.

Some of the more conspicuous folk features are florid melodic lines composed of small intervals, ancient modes and syncopated rhythms influenced by Mediterranean dances such as the Arabic *debka* and the Israeli *hora*.

During World War II and the War of Independence, most composers were cut off from musical developments in the outside world, and only in the late 1950s did interest grow in the newer styles and techniques. At that time new directions began to be perceived. Folk elements still predominated, but there was a definite tendency among younger composers to free themselves from the dance-like pastoral approach of their predecessors; they used folkloristic elements in a more dissonant and personal manner.

Although in the past some Israeli composers may have lacked close personal contact with developments abroad, today most are aware of musical events through radio, records, scores and publications, which come to Israel in great profusion from all over the world. Others even see an advantage in their geographical isolation from the centers of musical fashion as they strive for a music that is both distinctive and new.

Among the older group of European-trained composers, Paul Ben-Haim is the best known. Originally named Paul Frankenburger, Ben-Haim was born in Munich on July 5, 1897. Paul's mother Anna came from a totally assimilated family, most of whom had converted to Christianity. This was a common phenomenon in the Munich community and was a response by intellectual Jewish circles to emancipation. They were convinced that full emancipation was an integral part of political freedom and unity and that the Jewish religion was of secondary importance. [2] Paul's father, a successful lawyer, was a deeply religious man, but religiously undogmatic, and in the Frankenburger household none of the observances were kept. In a letter to Hirshberg Ben-Haim remembers, "My father used to go to synagogue regularly and often took me with him. Without him and that which he taught me from time to time, I would have been completely ignorant of Jewish tradition, but for all that, he was never dogmatic, for he was tolerant and open-minded in every way." [3]

Paul was a weak and sickly child, and it was some time before he developed the physical and emotional stamina which enabled him to cope with a staggering work load and live to be over eighty years of age. The doctors forbade him to attend school regularly, and his parents engaged private tutors for him. He made rapid progress, and after overcoming his sickliness and entering school two years late, he was admitted directly into fourth grade. A year later, he became a regular pupil at the Wilhelm-Gymnasium in Munich, receiving a typical humanistic education: religion, German, Latin, Greek, French, mathematics, history and physical education. In the first years the curriculum also included geography and science. His marks were always "Very Good" in religion and "Good" in other subjects, except for science and physical education, in which he was average. In his fourth year at primary school, his teacher maintained that he had no ear for music whatsoever, since he had been unable to sing any note that the teacher played for him. The teacher's assessment did not prevent his parents from providing him with music lessons. His mother was a good amateur pianist, and his older brother played in a youth orchestra. Deciding to take up the violin, his teacher tested him at the outset and discovered, to everyone's surprise, that he was gifted with perfect pitch. His progress was rapid, and after two years, he was playing a Mozart violin concerto, although the piano began to interest him more and more. He was eleven years old when he began to play the piano, which he later said attracted him because of the ability to play several voices simultaneously. At the same time he began to study harmony and counterpoint.

He graduated from the Academy of Music where he studied violin, piano, harmony, counterpoint and conducting. After his graduation he studied piano with Berthold Kellerman, a pupil of Liszt.[4] His composition teachers included Friederich Klose, a student of Anton Bruckner, and Walter Courvoisier, a prominent member of the "Müenchner Schule."[5]

Ben-Haim's creative life was comprised of two distinct periods. The first began in Germany after he completed his studies at the Academy in July 1920 where he worked as a conductor and composer. He was assistant conductor at the Munich State Opera (1920-1924) and conductor at the Augsburg Opera House (1924-1931).[6] These activities comprised the German period of his creative life.

In 1933, uprooted by Nazism, he emigrated to Palestine where the second period of his creative life began. In an interview with

Jay S. Harrison in the *New York Herald-Tribune* Ben-Haim says of his adopted country:

> Now, you must remember that in '33 Palestine was a British mandate and I was only able to obtain a tourist visa. That visa stipulated in strong terms that I was not allowed to do any work, even if it was offered to me. But I was asked to give recitals. I couldn't I answered. "Nonsense, my friends answered, give them, but change your name first. No one will know."
> So I decided to take a Hebrew name. As it happened, my father's name was Heinrich, Haim in Hebrew- it means "life," and "Ben" means "son of." So I took the name Ben-Haim, son of Heinrich. I must say I am glad. Frankenburger is too long, and too German in character. Ben-Haim suits me better.[7]

Ben-Haim described 1939 as a decisive year in his career as a composer. In that year, performances were held in Tel Aviv, of two of the most important works he had composed in Germany. The Palestine Philharmonic Orchestra played the "Concerto Grosso" and "Pan," a symphonic poem.[8] From 1949 to 1954 he was the Director of the Jerusalem Academy of Music and was its pedagogical advisor from 1960 to 1966. Ben-Haim was also president of the Israel Composers' Association.[9]

Through his study of A. Z. Idelsohn's books while still in Germany, he became acquainted with the Jewish and Arab folkloristic music tradition from the theoretical standpoint.[10] From 1939 to 1948 his collaboration with Bracha Zephirah, a well-known Israeli singer, familiarized him with regional traditions firsthand. For those nine years he was her accompanist and was greatly influenced by her, writing over sixty songs for her, based on Oriental folk melodies.[11]

Zephirah first went to see Paul Ben-Haim with a request for him to write instrumental accompaniments for her. Then he became interested in her folk music. She said:

> Ben-Haim is important as the bridge between starting a tradition of Israeli music, from a time when there was nothing, to the future of music in Israel. He combined European elements of music with aspects of indigenous traditional melodies. [12]

The music he began to create from the beginning of his residence in Palestine led to the establishment of what musical historians term "The Eastern-Mediterranean School" of Israeli composers, a school which Peter Gradenwitz has noted, attempts to incorporate "something of the Oriental-pastoral-Mediterranean spirit and to exploit by means of modern technique the Oriental style of melodic invention, rhythmic organization and instrumental coloration." The Mediterranean School was a movement generated in Palestine around the middle 1940s. The term was coined by Friedrich Nietzsche nearly a century before when he compared the lightness and charm of Bizet's "southern" music to that of Wagner's ponderous, Teutonic music dramas.

Ben-Haim was not a slavish folklorist; vernacular elements of ethnic music were digested into his compositional vocabulary much as in the case of Bartok. There is seldom direct quotation of folk melodies or rhythms in his works. Rather, like Bartok and Sibelius, he works creatively with themes and devices patterned closely after folk idioms, unless he clearly and carefully indicates usages of actual and authentic traditional material. The coloration of Near Eastern elements in his music added a new dimension to his expression.

Ben-Haim's surname as well as his music soon reflected his new national identity so his immigration to Palestine turned out to be the great turning point in his life. As he himself has said:

> Most people don't realize that Jews from Asia and Africa outnumber those from Europe in Israel. Jews from Yemen, Turkey, Iraq, Algeria, Egypt and Morocco have their own music, related to the Arabic, perhaps, but always

distinctive. Even before I went to Israel, I was interested in these musical traditions.[13]

One of the single most important aspects of Ben-Haim's music is the synthesis of Eastern and Western musical materials. He has written:

> I am of the West by birth and education, but I stem from the East and live in the East. I regard this as a great blessing indeed and it makes me feel grateful. The problem of a synthesis of East and West occupies musicians all over the world. If we — thanks to our living in a country that forms a bridge between East and West — can provide a modest contribution to such a synthesis in music, we shall be very happy.[14]

Ben-Haim was seeking a specifically Jewish style which began before his emigration to Palestine. Heinrich Schalit, a pianist, organist and composer living in Munich in the 1920s, is largely responsible for the infusion of Eastern elements into Ben-Haim's music. In 1921, Schalit heard a performance of Ben-Haim's String Quartet. When asked about this occasion, Schalit, who was living in Evergreen, Colorado, replied:

> When I heard compositions of Paul Frankenburger for the first time, I was greatly impressed by the remarkable maturity of his technique and style; he wrote in a contemporary vein — but with no trace of our ancestral Jewish heritage. As a conscious Jewish musician and Zionist, I considered it my duty to convince him of the necessity of devoting his talents to Jewish music and culture. I met Paul Frankenburger and we became friends. He became acquainted with my music and its Jewish idiom; he was deeply impressed and conducted my "Sacred Songs for Baritone and Orchestra" with much success in a concert.[15]

Thus, the Jewish spark in him was ignited and helped to prepare his career as Israel's foremost composer.

Through Schalit's suggestion, Ben-Haim undertook to study the works of Abraham Zvi Idelsohn, whose monumental *Hebraeischer-Orientalischer Melodienschatz* [16] unlocked the door to the melodies of the Jews of the Near East. He was thus introduced to the rich diversity of ancient modes. His first few years were spent in extensive travel through Palestine and its neighboring lands listening to and absorbing both the music of Jewish and Arabic communities. Much of the music he arranged for Bracha Zephirah was a result of this absorption. Zephirah was also a great influence on the composer's assimilation of the music of the Middle East.

Ben-Haim was also very much influenced by the theoretical writings of Paul Hindemith, and was in fact an ardent student and admirer of his works. Of Hindemith, Ben-Haim has written: "In my opinion, he is the greatest theoretician since Couperin. In 1955 I had a very interesting meeting with him in Zurich, a really unforgettable event." [17]

Opportunities arose to hear Hindemith's music, and while still in Germany, Ben-Haim conducted Hindemith's opera *Neues vom Tage* (*Today's News*) at the Augsburg Opera in 1930. Although the styles of the two composers are quite different, Hindemith's influence upon Ben-Haim is apparent in many compositions. These influences, having come from different corners of the earth, all work together to bring about the development of a style unique to Ben-Haim.

The composer died in Tel-Aviv in 1984 at the age of 87. In its obituary, Jon Pareles of the *New York Times* wrote:

> Paul Ben-Haim, a leading Israeli composer, died Saturday [January 20] in Tel Aviv.
> Mr. Ben-Haim's music reflected strong Israeli nationalism and an effort to synthesize Western classical forms with the sounds of Jewish and Middle Eastern folk music.
> During the 1940's and 50's Mr Ben-Haim became an influential composer in Israel and his works were frequently performed around the world. He

was the president of the Israeli Composers Association in the 1950's and received the Israel State Prize in 1957 for his work "The Sweet Psalmist of Israel."

Leonard Bernstein conducted the work's New York premier in 1959, with the New York Philharmonic. Harold C. Schonberg wrote in the New York Times, "Mr Ben-Haim's harmonies are mostly traditional, but his conception is unmistakably of this century."

Mr Ben-Haim later became honorary president of the Israeli Composers Union and head of the National Music Council. He was also on the advisory board of the Hebrew Arts School in New York City, which will present a memorial concert of his music on February 15th. His "Kabbalat Shabbat" (Friday evening service) received its New York premier at a 1968 Philharmonic Hall concert honoring the 20th anniversary of the founding of the state of Israel.

Mr. Ben-Haim is survived by his wife, Helena and his son Yoram.

Notes

1. John Vinton, *Dictionary of Contemporary Music*. (New York: E. P. Dutton, 1974).
2. Jehoash Hirshberg, *Paul Ben-Haim, His Life and Works*. (Tel-Aviv: Am Oved Publishers, 1989).
3. Hirshberg 197.
4. Aron Marko Rothmüller, *The Music of the Jews*. (South Brunswick, NJ: T. Yoseloff, 1960).
5. Richard Schaal, "Walter Courvoisier." *Die Musik in Geschichte un Gegenward*, part 18, 19; cols. 1752-53. (Kassel, W. Germany: Bärenreiter-Verlag, 1949).
6. Vinton 69.
7. Hirshberg 180.
8. Bruce Bohle, Ed., *The International Cyclopedia of Music and Musicians,* 10th ed. (New York: Dodd Mead and Co., 1975).
9. Vinton 169.
10. Peter Gradenwitz, *The Music of the Jews*. (New York: W.W. Norton & Company, Inc., 1949).
11. Judith L. Shiffers, "An Analysis of Selected Cello Compositions by Israeli Composers: The Synthesis of East and West." (Ph. D. dissertation, New York University, 1981).
12. Eric Salzman, *The New York Times*, May 24, 1959.
13. Paul Ben-Haim to Anita Hepner, December 29, 1970. Anita Hepner, "The Vocal Works of Paul Ben-Haim." (Master's Thesis, Queens College, New York, 1972).
14. Heinrich Schalit to Anita Hepner, January 16, 1971. Hepner. 39
15. Abraham Zvi Idelsohn, *Hebraeischer-Orientalischer Melodenschatz*, 12 Vols. (Berlin: Haerz, 1914-1932).
16. Paul Ben-Haim, private interview with Anita Hepner in Tel Aviv, March, 1970. Hepner, p. 120.
17. Hepner, p. 138.

Chapter Two

SONATINA OP. 38

This work is in three movements marked allegretto *grazzioso*, *Improvvisazione*, and *Molto vivo*, the latter a toccata movement with the headlong drive of a perpetual motion machine. Outstanding among Ben-Haim's piano compositions, *Sonatina* is a prime example of Eastern Mediterranean music; with its lyricism and dance-like qualities, Ben-Haim's pastoral spirit is evident. It is a good example of his Oriental-sounding melodies and Western harmonies, although the harmonies are not always traditional, and in fact contain elements of impressionistic sound effects.

The immediate model for this work is Ravel's *Sonatine* (1905), which was inspired by an interest in tones, textures and concepts of formal classicism. Ben-Haim does not compose a psudo Neo-Classic movement, but instead presents an organic, energetic form whose main objective is a balance between tonal stability and movement, between uniformity and contrast. Likewise Ben-Haim's work is characterized by a clarity of organization and the avoidance of powerful emotional expression."[1]

Within each movement, the sections are fairly clean-cut as explained in the following discussion. Two noted pianists and pedagogues, James Friskin and Erwin Freundlich, have said in part:

> These piano works [including "Sonatina"] have been acclaimed by listeners and pianists alike as unique contributions to the modern keyboard repertoire. They are expertly written for the instrument and contain music that is warm, lyrical, colorful and filled with exotic traits derived from Oriental music. [Ben-Haim] also displays a real flair for the keyboard.[2]

First Movement

Stylistic Level

Sonority

The over-all impression of the first movement's sonority is subdued. It begins softly and ends dying away to a whisper on the piano's lowest note, marked *pppp*. There is only one *fortissimo* at m. 53, just before the recapitulation and this is built up to by six measures of *forte*. This represents the outstanding climax of the movement. The recapitulation itself is marked *ppp* in striking contrast to what came before.

Another kind of climax occurs at the end of the exposition, where the melodic line rises, but the dynamic level falls to a *pianississimo*.

Ben-Haim frequently uses *subito piano* after loud or forceful passages. Examples of this are found at the beginning of the transition (mm. 13-14) and several times during the development at mm. 42-43 and 43-44.

In contrast to the general clarity of the texture, the recapitulation represents a striking difference in sonority, being infused with an impressionistic haze, achieved by pedaled diatonic scales.

Harmony

The prevailing tonality is rooted in the Aeolian mode which is strongly established in the very first measure and reestablished in the last measure of the movement. As in traditional sonata form, the key of the Second Theme is in the dominant, first introduced at m. 21. Ben-Haim shows a marked tendency towards using open fourths and fifths, strikingly apparent during the development section (m. 43).

Rhythm

Allegretto grazzioso is suggestive of the pastoral character of this particular work and of Ben-Haim's style in general. The meter is largely unchanged except for several places where it shifts from quadruple to duple — fundamentally not a real change at all. However, the beat fluctuates considerably, with a ritard often coming at the end of a phrase or section. At the beginning of the Coda (m. 95) there is a basic tempo change (*piu calmo*), with an *accelerando* and Tempo I reestablishing the original *Allegretto* marking.

A salient feature of the rhythmic scheme is the use of syncopation; this is found at every appearance of the Principal Theme, and is also an integral feature of the Second Theme.

Melody

The most obvious melodic feature in this first movement is the use of the descending octave skip which forms the basis of the Principal Theme and is a binding motivic device. It is a striking idea, cropping up again and again during the course of the movement. It is easy to hear no matter where or in what context it appears.

Although the melody has a Middle-Eastern flavor with its frequent embellishments and shifting major and minor modes, much of the phrasing follows a regular two-bar pattern and is outstanding for its lyrical quality and impressionistic coloring.

Structural Level

Clarity

In this opening movement, phrase structure is clearly delineated and phrase lengths are predictable through the nearly consistent use of four-measure periods. The composer also enhances the divisions of structural elements through the use of commas, which indicate "breathing" spaces.

Proportion

Ben-Haim's handling of the sonata form in this work is masterful. The divisions of the movement into Exposition, Development, Recapitulation and Coda are clear-cut and easy to perceive on a purely listening level. Within these sections, first theme, transition, second theme and closing material are also clearly delineated.

The biggest climax — that of the preparation for the recapitulation (m. 53) — comes very nearly in the middle of the movement, since there are 110 measures in the piece.

Dynamic climaxes, both loud and soft, are strategically placed, coming as they do at the ends of significant structural members. These climaxes are often accompanied by a slackening of the ongoing pulse, immediately followed by an a tempo mark.

Integrity

The piece is highly integrated through the consistent use of the descending (sometimes ascending) octave skip, which opens this work. It forms the basis for the transition, much of the development and the entire coda. In other words, the musical elements are interrelated to the point that they function expressively in an organized musical environment.

Complexity

In the large context, the Primary and Secondary Themes represent a strong contrast. The Primary Theme is disjunct and staccato, while the Second Theme (m. 21) is conjunct and legato. Textures in the exposition and recapitulation are more transparent than in the development section. There is also the tendency to use the upper register of the keyboard in those two sections which contrasts with the wider range of registers in the development.

Ben-Haim is extremely frugal in the use of his material. There are only three distinctly different musical ideas: the Principal Theme, the Second Theme (m. 21) and the closing material (m. 30).

Subtlety

Ben-Haim's skillful manipulation of the sonata form leads the listener easily and naturally from one musical event to the next. There are few surprises in terms of sudden outbursts of fortissimo, or strange or unexpected chord progressions. The one spot which confounds the listener's expectations is at the recapitulation where the Primary Theme is accompanied by upward-rushing scales with the damper pedal held down. This gives the passage an uncharacteristic blur of sound.

Second Movement

Stylistic Level

Sonority

The first measure is marked *mezzo forte*. About halfway through the piece there is a *forte* marking which started building at m. 28 exactly in the middle of the piece. This climax concludes at m. 33 with the last measure of the work, m. 47 marked with four *p*'s. The general dynamic outline is *forte*, and then *pppp*. However, there are many indications other than these.

Although the first measure is marked *mezzo forte*, the second measure is already marked *piano,* and then we have *mezzo piano* at m. 3, piano at m. 5 and *pianissimo* at m. 9. The point is that the piece is generally soft, in keeping with Ben-Haim's characteristically gentle sounds.

At *calmo* (m. 14) a new section is marked *piano* again. There is the special effect of *subito piano* (m.23), and another *sforzando* to *pianissimo* (m. 35), in terms of sudden dynamic changes. The closeness and the repetition of the notes especially in the beginning of this movement, seem to tend toward the human voice — almost a cantorial chant. However, starting at m. 23, the rolled chords and the broken octaves in the bass remind one of a harp.

Ben-Haim often uses the device of unison writing at climaxes and such is the case in this movement. This is shown at m. 33 with the high B-flats in unison and then with a reprise of the opening theme at m. 34, which is the climax of the movement.

The thickest texture in the movement is found in the middle section; the beginning and ending are much thinner and more transparent.

Harmony

Although there are nebulous areas of E-flat major in m. 2, C-flat major in m. 4 and A-flat major in m. 6, and then again E-flat major in m. 12, it is much clearer that Ben-Haim is in C minor in the *calmo* section at m. 14. There is also a B-flat pedal in m. 36 through 38 with a definite implication of B-flat major. In the last four measures, he seems to oscillate between C minor and E-flat major, with a much stronger emphasis on C minor, the tonality which ends the piece.

Starting at m. 24 there is a marked tendency for the composer to double the fourths in the bass and create chords that way. The writing is more linear in the beginning, homophonic in the middle (m. 26), and then linear again towards the end.

Rhythm

Although the time signature changes frequently, these changes are not significant because 9/8 and 3/4 are both triple meters. However, the meter does shift from triple to quadruple when it goes into 12/8. Ben-Haim continues to put *rallentando* or *ritenuto* at the end of significant sections, such as m. 13, right before the *calmo*. This expanding is also implied in m. 32. before a return to Tempo I, and at the end (m. 44), where he writes *rit. molto*. He also continues the rhythmic idea of syncopation heard in the very first measure of the *Improvvisazione*, making that idea more tangible.

Melody

The most salient feature of the melody in this movement is actually a contrasting idea. The opening measure has one note (B-flat) repeated. In the next measure there is a melismatic variant of the B-flat, with written out ornamentation, rapid, like the chirping of a bird; the two measures create a direct contrast to each other. This opening melody is reminiscent of a shepherd playing his pipes in biblical Palestine.

The next outstanding melodic feature is m. 14 in the bass. This cello-like melody is then picked up by the right hand in m. 16 in canonic fashion. Again there are shifting major and minor modes and embellishments which produce an Oriental flavor.

Structural Level

Clarity

In order to produce a feeling of improvisation in this work, the composer structures his phrases less symmetrically than in the previous movement. This is accomplished through the use of frequent meter changes. For example, in the first section, consisting of 13 measures, there are five meter changes and the next section, m. 14, begins in still a new meter, 3/4.

This movement divides itself into three sections which are clearly indicated by obvious tempo changes. For example, m. 14, which begins the middle section, is marked *calmo* and the composer provides a new metronome setting. The return of the first section, m. 33, is marked Tempo I.

Proportion

The shape and divisions in this improvisation are very clear. The first section is mm. 1 to 13. The second section starting at the *Calmo*, is mm. 14 to 39 which is 26 measures long. The closing material, mm. 40 to 47, is 8 measures long.

The music begins quietly and builds intensely to just past the center of the piece and then dissolves back into the *dolce* section at m. 36. Eventually there is a *morendo* marked at m. 43. This movement, like the first and third, presents a musical architecture that reflects the thematic conception of an arch. The return at m. 40 to the opening material breathes out a haunting refrain that ends in a whisper.

Integrity

What unifies this piece is the balance of motivic repetition and contrast, as expressed earlier in the first and second measures. The germ of the idea is the repeated B-flat, however, out of which everything seems to grow. All the elements are working together to produce a unified effect. It is actually the third measure, a continuation of the opening idea, which is picked up in m. 15 in order to introduce the next major idea at *calmo*. This is expanded upon until the climax at m. 33 which is the result of a logical and cohesive design. All the ideas are woven together from within and from without.

Complexity

The first two measures represent a marked contrast to each other. However, there is also a strong distinction between the opening theme, with its bird-like call and highly embellished line and the theme at m. 14 with its expansive melody in the bass; yet all these musical ideas grow out of each other.

Although it seems as though the composer is using fewer ornaments in the middle section, at mm. 24-26 those broken and rolled chords may be heard as types of embellishments. There is also a much thicker texture in the writing of the middle section than is found at both the beginning and the end.

If one had to assign orchestral instruments to this piece, perhaps a flute and a cello would be appropriate. Again, Ben-

Haim is quite frugal in his use of melodic material as there are only two main themes that he employs: one in the first two measures and one at m. 14, yet he weaves a lyrical rainbow of sound out of these simple motifs.

Subtlety

There are not too many deviations from the norm in this movement. However, it comes as a surprise that the climax in m. 33, after building up to this point, concludes with a unison recapitulation of the opening idea marked *molto forte*.

It is evident that one of Ben-Haim's stylistic devices is to strip a musical idea to its bare essence at a crucial point; thus making less mean more. As the writing gets more complex starting at m. 32 three staves are used.

Third Movement

Stylistic Level

Sonority

Although this movement is for the most part subdued, there is a quiet intensity which builds to several stunning moments of *forte* and *fortissimo* and eventually triple *forte* at the very end. Where the range is scale-wise and narrow, such as at the beginning, the dynamics are softer. As the range widens, the dynamics are amplified apace. Also, the music becomes louder as the density of the texture gets thicker, as at m. 62 where it starts building to the big climax at m. 69. There are several places where Ben-Haim uses *forte-piano* such as mm. 9 and 11. Also there are instances of the use of *sforzando* on one note or chord which the previous phrase has built up to; for example mm. 19-20, 28, 30-31, etc. Starting at m. 66 there is almost constant excitement and climaxes within climaxes for the next two pages until the music starts winding down at m. 98. The louder passages usually occur at the opening of significant sections; mm. 21, 66 and 89 are the beginnings of new ideas.

Harmony

The prevailing mode of this movement seems to be the key of A minor. It only seems to be in A minor because Ben-Haim tends toward bi-tonality. The very first note in the right hand is an A but there is an E-flat and B-flat, an open fifth, in the bass. If they were played together it would be a tone cluster. This movement is in the Aeolian mode because the leading-tone, G-sharp does not appear, except for brief, insignificant moments.

The next important tonality is C minor at m. 58. However, for the most part the tonality implies the Aeolian mode. An example of this can be found at the end of the movement, where there is an a octave in the bass and then a tone cluster emphasizing the note A.

Interspersed throughout the piece, there is frequent use of open fifths in the bass from the beginning to the end, while in contrast, the right hand often has scale-wise passages.

Rhythm

The tempo and rhythm of this movement are in marked contrast to the *Improvvisazione* that came before. The second movement required a very free flowing rhythm with a liberal use of rubato. This movement, on the other hand, has a propulsive forward drive similar to the works of Liszt, and is marked *molto vivo*. The performer must have a strong internal beat in order not to rush.

There are several instances (mm. 38 and 48) where Ben-Haim marks *modestamente marcato* in this movement, which directs the pianist not to play it too strictly. The other main tempo indications are the *molto vivo* in the beginning, *un poco meno mosso* at m. 58, the *accelerando* at m. 62, Tempo I at m. 66, and finally the *presto* at m. 115.

The *molto vivo* is suggestive of the intensity this movement requires, almost like a whirling dervish from the very beginning. The new syncopated rhythm introduced in m. 13 with its rest-play-rest-play pattern, recalls the ancient, national dance of Israel, the *hora*.

Un poco meno mosso introduces a completely new section, the *hora* rhythm again, with a sensual atmosphere, conjuring up visions of the dance of the seven veils. This contrast is brief, because at Tempo I, the perpetual motion drive returns.

The coda, marked *presto*, begins with quiet intensity and then builds to furious excitement up to the concluding chord.

Melody

The outstanding feature of the melody in this movement is its scale-wise motion and the feeling that it is a written-out ornament. The motion of the melody together with the open fifths in the bass is a binding motivic device throughout this work.

The second theme occurs in m. 13 with the new *hora* rhythm. Here the register is much higher. At m. 38 is another form of the melody. At *Un poco meno mosso*, m. 58, the rhythm is the important element in the music and melodic considerations are less obvious. Again, although the melody sounds Middle Eastern with its frequent embellishment and shifting major and minor modes as before, much of the phrasing follows a regular four bar pattern.

Clarity

The beginning of this movement has a perpetual motion effect created by a steady scale-wise 16th note movement which gradually expands intervalically. In direct contrast to this idea, at *Un poco meno mosso,* m. 58, the alternating chords in right and left hand produce a markedly disjunct result which eventually wends its way back to the perpetual motion idea and a thicker texture.

The *Presto* coda, consisting of "blind" octaves is preceded by a morendo dynamic effect and several beats of silence.

Proportion

Ben-Haim divides this work into four sections, *Molto vivo*, *Un poco meno mosso*, Tempo I and *Presto*. The section marked *Un poco meno mosso* is completely new material, whereas Tempo I is an expansion of that material. Dynamic climaxes both loud and soft continue to be strategically placed coming at the end of significant sections.

The comparative lengths of each movement are not symmetrical. The first movement is the longest, the middle movement the shortest, and the last movement is two-thirds the length of the first.

Integrity

The main motivic device which binds this piece together is the scale-wise melody introduced in the very beginning, together with the open fifths in the bass. This is exploited in many different ways through out the work and forms the basis for the transition, much of the development and the closing material, while the *hora* rhythm is an important binding factor. Therefore the scale-wise writing and the syncopated, leaping intervals that are integrating the work are the contrasting ideas. All these musical elements functioning together produce coherence and unit.

Complexity

In the large context the first and second themes represent a strong contrast. The primary theme is mainly conjunct and legato while the second theme is largely disjunct and staccato. The section with the thickest texture comes in the middle at Tempo I. As mentioned above, Ben-Haim is quite frugal in his use of melodic material. There are only two different musical ideas; the Primary Theme and the Secondary Theme, at m. 13.

Subtlety

There are not many spots which are unpredictable but one which does strike the listener is at m. 32. It is suddenly in a rather low register, and the composer asks the performer to hold a low D-flat and keep the pedal down while playing a very chromatic and close-knit—almost an *ostinato* bass—for quite some time. Another spot is the climax Ben-Haim achieves at m. 91 where he uses unison melody again. After so much has been happening he suddenly does less to achieve more, as mentioned above. Also the *presto* is a surprise with the broken octaves up to the end. The mere fact that this movement is to be played so furiously and *con fuoco*, is in itself rather uncharacteristic of Ben-Haim's writing.

SONATINA, SECOND MOVEMENT

SONATINA, THIRD MOVEMENT

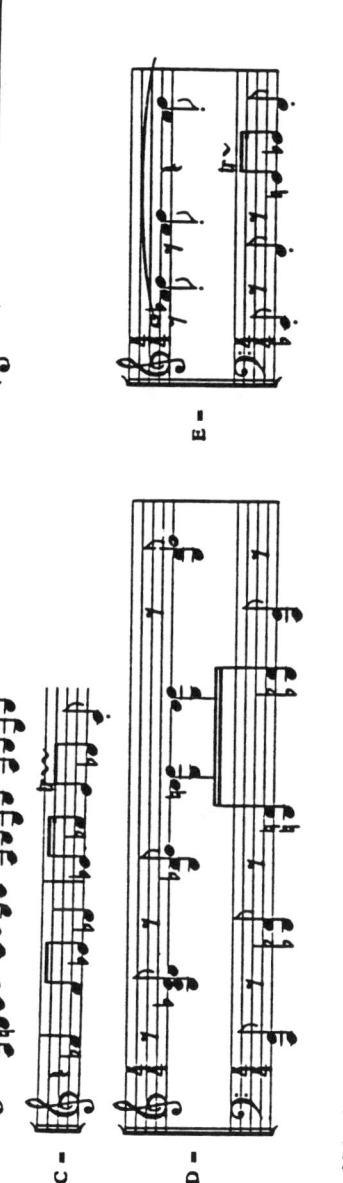
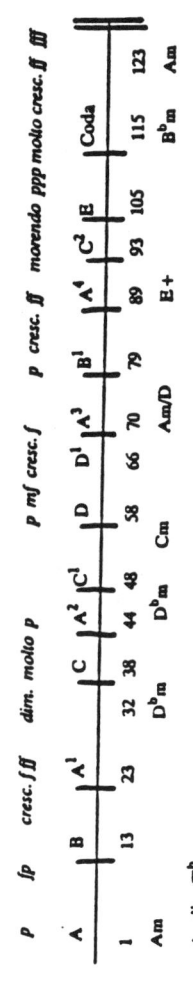

Notes

1. Jehoash Hirshberg, *Paul Ben-Haim, His Life and Works*. (Tel Aviv: Am Oved Publishers, 1989).
2. James Friskin and Irwin Freundlich, *Music for the Piano*. (New York: Holt, Rinehart and Winston, Inc., 1954).

Chapter Three
FIVE PIECES FOR PIANO OP. 34

This work has been acclaimed by pianists and listeners alike as a unique contribution to the modern keyboard repertoire. They are expertly written for the instrument and contain music that is "warm, lyrical, colorful and filled with exotic traits derived from oriental music. The popular *Toccata* has a style which is indebted to the toccata from Ravel's *Le Tombeau de Couperin*."[1]

Pastorale

Stylistic Level

Sonority

In this opening work there is no *forte* and in fact, an impressionistic haze of sound created with the use of the pentatonic scale. The loudest that it gets is *mezzo forte* at mm. 22 and 27. Ben-Haim produces a subtle intensity by working within these various degrees of softness. *Pastorale* begins *mezzo piano* in the right hand and piano in the left. Shortly thereafter at m.7 it becomes *pianissimo* and *lontano* and at m. 14 *poco a poco diminuendo*. In recalling the opening theme at m. 29, there is a triple *piano* marking which implies a suggestion of the beginning rather than an actual reprise. It ends with four *p*'s in the last measure and in the very first measure there is an indication of *non troppo dolce* — not too sweet. The composer perhaps thought that with these very soft markings that there might be a tendency to play in a superficial or sentimental manner, which is definitely not what he intended.

Because the range of this music for the most part is narrow, it gives it a *cantabile* quality, and there are even commas in various places for "breathing." Like other works of this genre, the movement fades away in an impressionistic cloud.

Harmony

The melody in the first two measures strongly suggests bitonality together with a bagpipe drone in the left hand, which starts as dissonant seconds and adds notes creating a cluster. Although it appears to have elements of both pentatonic and whole-tone scales, the work clearly ends in A minor with an added F-sharp. This tonal ambiguity prevails throughout the whole piece with a very strong feeling of A minor in the right hand and major seconds added for coloristic effect in the left. The last measure ends with a fermata on A, seeming to finally establish the elusive tonality of A, but even here the tonality is obscured by the final chord with its additional F-sharp and D.

Rhythm

In Ben-Haim's style there is a feeling of spontaneity, an improvisatory character which is prevalent in many of his works, and indeed is part of the tempo indication of this work. Although rubato is definitely called for in performance it must not be overdone and it should be noted that the meter only changes in one measure (m. 16) at the climax of the first section. Here the expansion of the motif is at its broadest and the effect is enhanced by the word *calando*, stretching the four beats to their maximum. *A tempo* at m. 16 is reinforced by a *marcato* marking.

Melody

The most obvious melodic feature of this first movement is the use of a scale-wise, pentatonic melody in antecedent-consequent fashion in the first two measures.

Example 1. *Pastorale,* mm.1-2

This is certainly a binding motivic device, used throughout the entire piece. The melodic content consists of motivic fragments, the most distinguishable features being the pentatonic scale-wise melody, the antecedent-consequent phrasing and the expanded embellishment of the opening motif as mentioned above.

Within the large-scale embellishment of this melody there are also small mordents interspersed throughout, giving it an oriental flavor. The constant forward movement and lyricism clashes with the major seconds and cluster-like chords in the bass. The polyphonic texture and counter melody in m. 17 grows out of the intimate interweaving of the melodic ideas which came before.

Structural Level

Clarity

The three distinct sections in this movement are set forth by tempo changes. Between the first and second parts, there is also a comma, indicating a breathing pause. Between the second and third parts, there is a silent break created by a fermata over a quarter-note rest.

Proportion

The architectural design of this piece underscores the remarkable symmetry encountered in many of Ben-Haim's works. The first section is 16 measures and the last, starting at *piu lento* is 8, with the middle section being 11 measures. There is certainly a Germanic feel to this exact symmetry and indeed Ben-Haim was taught in Germany. This work is in ternary form; Section A being the first 16 measures, Section B the 11 measures marked a tempo, and A prime the *piu lento* section starting at m. 29. Dynamic climaxes are again strategically placed, coming at ends of significant sections marked with a slower tempo and then immediately after ward, *a tempo*.

This movement and the *Canzonetta* are the two shortest works in the Suite, and the only ones in ternary form.

Integrity

The interweaving of rhythmic, dynamic and melodic elements lend unity to this miniature. There is an internal drama which drives towards the center section of the piece. The development is quite organic and one section flows into the next. After a cascade of sound is heard at *piu lento* m. 29, we hear one or two colors again as the texture thins and the patterns spill down into a dreamy fog.

Complexity

In the larger context, the primary and secondary themes represent a strong contrast. The primary theme is conjunct, lyrical and flowing, despite the clashing bass. The second theme at a tempo m. 17 is more assertive, with its counter melodies and marcato marking, as well as frequent use of accented and ornamented notes. Therefore the touch needs to be different; more firm and articulated in this secondary material. The textures are also more transparent in the first section than in the second. Again, the composer is extremely frugal in his use of melodic material, with only two distinctly different musical ideas; the primary theme at the opening and the secondary theme at m. 17.

Intermezzo

Subtlety

The march-like theme at *a tempo*, although it grows out of the opening material is almost a surprise in its distinct change of mood from what came before. It is a mood of determination, of forward motion. There is a very effective moment at m. 28 when the entire section trails off into nothingness, the mood prolonged by a fermata. The use of contrapuntal material imbues this music with subtle inflections which become apparent only with repeated hearings.

Stylistic Level

Sonority

The term "intermezzo" is defined in the *Harvard Dictionary* as: "A 19th Century character piece, suggestive of a somewhat casual origin of the piece, as if it were composed between works of greater importance." Upon close inspection this certainly does seem to be the case. Although there are contrasting sections within the work, its general character is subdued; there is only in instance of *mezzo forte* at m. 29 with few climatic moments. It begins softly and ends by fading away to a whisper, with only a major second rippling the still water. There is only one main climax and that is the *mezzo forte* section mentioned above which is built up to from m. 24 in canonic fashion. Where the writing gets denser, starting at m. 33 and continuing to m. 38, the music builds to a second climax, although the *pianissimo* dynamic level is maintained. There are characteristic parallel fourths and fifths to be found in this section. The opening indications, *Trasognato*, which means "dreamy" along with *quasi allegretto* say a great deal about how this piece should be executed; the performer must create a dreamy, impressionistic haze of sound.

Harmony

The first few measures introduce an immediate clash in the harmony. The right hand points to A-flat major, while the left hand refers to E-flat minor, creating bi-tonality which is characteristic of Ben-Haim's writing. Although A-flat major seems to win out at the conclusion of the piece, there is that rumbling major second — A-flat, B-flat — in the bass in the last measure against a clear A-flat major chord. This harmony does in fact mesh completely with Ben-Haim's concept of dreaminess; it is found in every aspect of the work.

Rhythm

The *allegretto grazioso* is still suggestive of the pastoral character which permeates much of Ben-Haim's output. The meter is largely unchanged except for several places where it shifts from 9/8 to 12/8 and back to 9/8 which still maintains triple meter — not a drastic change after all. The beat fluctuates with a ritard coming at the end of a phrase or section.

Throughout the movement there is an abundance of markings referring to tempo, which gives the piece the character of an improvisation. The rhythmic scheme is also enhanced by the use of syncopation and polyrhythms. It is featured at every appearance of the principal theme.

Melody

The most outstanding melodic attribute of this second movement, which resembles a *Siciliano*, (defined in the Performance Guide) is the use of the downward skip of a descending fifth which forms the basis of the principal theme and is a unifying motivic device. This is easy for the listener to hear at all times.

Example 2. *Intermezzo*, mm. 1-2.

The next melodic element is the opening of the second theme at m. 6 which employs the use of an ascending octave skip, also easy to hear. There are three themes which unify this movement. The opening descending fifth, the ascending octave and the running sixteenth-notes which form the transitional material found in mm. 4, 21 and 41. This idea contrasts strongly with the other two.

Structural Level

Clarity

The large sections in this piece are introduced by changes in tempo; they are usually preceded by such directions as *rubato* or *calando*. The melody which is introduced at a tempo (m. 6), is transferred to the bass at m. 24 of the middle section. The dreamy opening, consisting of more spacious intervals is abruptly interrupted by a 16th note sextuplet at m. 4, which contrasts completely with the opening idea. The 16th note passage is later expanded upon at mm. 21-23 and functions as a bridge between the first and second sections.

Proportion

The design of this movement is often related to the opening motif at the beginning of the piece. It is also bound together by several related sections. M. 1 is A, m. 6 is B, m. 21, C, m. 24 B, M. 32 A', m. 39, an inversion of A, and the closing material from m. 42 is derived from the motif at m. 4. The introduction is constructed of 5 measures before a tempo, and the closing material (m. 42) also consists of 5 measures. One wonders if the composer did this on purpose or if it was a reflection of his instinctive need for order and proportion.

The biggest climax, the preparation for the restatement of the opening subject at m. 32, comes very nearly in the middle of the movement. Since the opening material is found in four places with contrasting ideas in between, it has many similarities to rondo form.

These motifs are stated as strongly interrelated themes and combine to unify this piece.

This *Intermezzo* along with the *Capriccio Agitato* is the next longest movement after the *Pastorale* and *Canzonetta*.

Canzonetta

Integrity

This piece is unified motivically through the consistent use of the descending (sometimes ascending) skip of a fifth, as well as he ascending skip of an octave which starts the second theme. These two themes, together with the transitional section consisting of sixteenth-note runs, unify the whole piece. The coordination of musical elements within sections of individual movements is far more consistently applied than the concinnity that exists between the movements themselves.

Complexity

In the larger picture the primary and secondary themes do not represent a tremendous contrast. They both have skips of a fifth or larger; one is descending and one ascending, which is the only contrast between them. However, the transitional material, the 16th note runs mentioned above, is not only different from what came before, but almost sounds like it belongs in another piece. Yet all these elements combine to work together to form a work of unity and beauty.

The texture, which was thinner previously, becomes more complex starting at a tempo, m. 24, and also introduces the contrapuntal activity.

Subtlety

There is not too much here that departs from the norm. The use of the transitional material (the 16th-note runs) is very far removed from the opening material, and almost sound as though it came from another piece, nevertheless it works and is effective within this context. The only other place where there is a touch of the unexpected is in the very last measure where A-flat is firmly established; suddenly there is the major 2nd rumbling in the bass, throwing off the sense of tonality.

Capriccio Agitato

Stylistic Level

Sonority

"Cappricio" is defined in the *Harvard Dictionary* as, "a title for a composition of a capricious or humorous character." The title of this piece quite properly describes its mood: agitated and capricious. However, the forward propulsion and the sheer tempestuousness of this work do not suggest a humorous idiom but point more to *agitato* rather than *capriccio*. Most of the piece is marked *forte* or *fortissimo* with only a few sections interspersed marked *piano* or *pianissimo*. These soft markings usually appear at the beginning of important sections; m. 14 and m. 30 for example.

The opening, with its pentatonic and whole-tone scales undulating in a wave-like manner, creates a sonorous cloud of sound. This idea of a great rumbling sound is further exploited at m. 14 where Ben-Haim indicates that the pedal is to be used. It is only at m. 5, with the sharply accented chords articulating the splashes of sound, that a more distinct tone quality is required. The loudest portion of the piece, which is also its main climax begins at m. 52. Because of its thickness of texture and intensity of sound, the section starting at m. 14 is also a climax, and is the densest portion of the whole work.

Harmony

Ben-Haim uses the pentatonic scale in his running 32nd-note passages in m. 1. He hovers around certain modes such as the Aeolian in m. 10 and the dominant minor starting at m. 14; However, he clearly ends the movement in A major. The chords he uses throughout the piece show a marked tendency to combine both fourths and fifths. If one plays the right hand alone at m. 5 the chords produce an ancient quality suggesting organum, while if one adds the open fourths in the left hand, a contemporary sound is created. The texture is predominantly homophonic; chordal passages alternating with clouds of impressionistic coloring which are provided by the sixteenth-note arpeggios.

Rhythm

The triple meter is quite regularly maintained in spite of mm. 6, 25-26 and 53, where there is a brief change to duple meter. At m. 25-26 there is a climax whose effect is enhanced by the broadening into quadruple and then duple meter. The movement alternates between improvisatory, impressionistic waves of sound and sharp, *marcato* chordal passages.

Melody

There is one melodic idea in this movement. The first time it is heard is in the top notes of the parallel motion chords introduced at m. 5.

Example 3. *Cappricio Agitato*, m. 5

It continues, more broadly drawn out at m. 16, and sings out above the swirling tumult of sound from the sixteenth-note arpeggios below. It is further developed at m. 40 and in effect, is continued on to the end of the piece.

Structural Level

Clarity

This movement has more continuity, unlike its predecessors, and is much more integrated; it does not break down as distinctly into contrasting sections as the others do. There is also much less use of tempo changes to delineate the few contrasting sections that there are. At m. 16, the composer brings together his two main ideas through the use of melodic material derived from m. 6, singing above a flowing arpeggiated bass pattern.

Proportion

Ben-Haim structures this work by giving much more space to accommodate the arpeggiated figurations, while the chordal patterns, used to contrast this material, take up fewer measures. The undulating scale runs which open the work give way to upward rushing broken chords and scales in the left hand at m. 10.

A little more than halfway through the piece, at m. 40, a new treatment of this main melodic idea is introduced which uses fragments of the theme starting at m. 5. The most intense climax of the piece comes nearly at the end at m. 61 and continues

Harmony

Ben-Haim uses the pentatonic scale in his running 32nd-note passages in m. 1. He hovers around certain modes such as the Aeolian in m. 10 and the dominant minor starting at m. 14; However, he clearly ends the movement in A major. The chords he uses throughout the piece show a marked tendency to combine both fourths and fifths. If one plays the right hand alone at m. 5 the chords produce an ancient quality suggesting organum, while if one adds the open fourths in the left hand, a contemporary sound is created. The texture is predominantly homophonic; chordal passages alternating with clouds of impressionistic coloring which are provided by the sixteenth-note arpeggios.

Rhythm

The triple meter is quite regularly maintained in spite of mm. 6, 25-26 and 53, where there is a brief change to duple meter. At m. 25-26 there is a climax whose effect is enhanced by the broadening into quadruple and then duple meter. The movement alternates between improvisatory, impressionistic waves of sound and sharp, *marcato* chordal passages.

Melody

There is one melodic idea in this movement. The first time it is heard is in the top notes of the parallel motion chords introduced at m. 5.

Example 3. *Cappricio Agitato*, m. 5

It continues, more broadly drawn out at m. 16, and sings out above the swirling tumult of sound from the sixteenth-note arpeggios below. It is further developed at m. 40 and in effect, is continued on to the end of the piece.

Structural Level

Clarity

This movement has more continuity, unlike its predecessors, and is much more integrated; it does not break down as distinctly into contrasting sections as the others do. There is also much less use of tempo changes to delineate the few contrasting sections that there are. At m. 16, the composer brings together his two main ideas through the use of melodic material derived from m. 6, singing above a flowing arpeggiated bass pattern.

Proportion

Ben-Haim structures this work by giving much more space to accommodate the arpeggiated figurations, while the chordal patterns, used to contrast this material, take up fewer measures. The undulating scale runs which open the work give way to upward rushing broken chords and scales in the left hand at m. 10.

A little more than halfway through the piece, at m. 40, a new treatment of this main melodic idea is introduced which uses fragments of the theme starting at m. 5. The most intense climax of the piece comes nearly at the end at m. 61 and continues unabated until the finish. Compared to the other movements in this suite, this is so far the most intense and stormy in character.

Integrity

One thematic idea, first announced at m. 5, runs through this work and ties it together. It is also unified through the use of the running accompaniment, which is balanced by parallel chords built up of fifths and fourths. This undulating accompaniment, often nebulous and ambiguous, gives way to the clarity and determination of the melodic chordal passages; herein lies the essence of this movement's design.

Complexity

Although there is only one theme from beginning to end, contrast is achieved through the use a 16th-note rushing accompaniment which sometimes articulates and sometimes underlies this melodic idea. There is also a dichotomy between the complexity of the rushing scale-wise figure and the straightforward simplicity of the parallel chordal passages.

Through the use of contrasting registers, another level of contrast is achieved. The opening statement of the theme (m. 5) is in the middle register; its continuation (m. 16) is in a lower register, and its final statement (m. 61) is in the upper reaches of the key board.

Subtlety

The combination of a long-lined melody, using many tied half-notes and dotted half-notes against a very fast-moving accompaniment is an unusual effect and a difficult one to achieve technically. Ben-Haim asks for the pedal only where the accompaniment becomes broken chords, and that, by inference, he does not want a blurred effect with the opening pentatonic scale passages.

A significant detail is the orchestral thinking behind the indication quasi trombe at m. 52

Canzonetta

Stylistic Level

Sonority

The *Canzonetta* is a lyrical song which comes between two turbulent outer movements. It provides an interlude, a point of repose between the two fiery outer movements, the Capriccio and the brilliant Toccata. Dynamically, the loudest part of this movement, which is also the climax, occurs at m. 25, and is the second half of the second section. Another climactic point is the last chord marked with four *p*'s. Thus the dynamics range of this work extends from *mezzo piano* to the superlative indication of softness, *pppp*.

The texture of much of this piece is chordal with a flowing, arpeggiated bass, implying a nocturne in the style of Chopin. The contrasting section starting at m. 17 is essentially a rhythmic and melodic variation on the opening. Although the bass is simpler, the melody is more florid and more embellished; the chords in the opening are quite full and rich. Also the range is noteworthy as it starts out in the middle range of the piano and at m.9 there is the same melody with added notes an octave higher and is marked *pianissimo* as opposed to *piano*.

As the emotional intensity increases, the register gets higher, such as mm. 9 and 25. The expression marks are also a clue to the sonority of this work. *Andante affettuoso* indicates that it should be played with warmth and affection; *molto dolce e cantando* implies a sweetly singing style. At m. 17 *amoroso* is indicated which suggests a love song.

Harmony

The harmonic scheme of this piece is simple to follow. From m. 1 to m. 16 it is clearly in the key of A minor (with an added F-sharp), and it ends in that tonality. From m. 17 it is in the dominant, E major. The piece is mainly homophonic in texture, however, at m. 36 the lines in the left hand part are more independent and there is some quasi-contrapuntal activity between those voices. Also, there is a tendency to oscillate between minor and major, or vice versa. For example, the opening soprano notes with the tenuto marks, E, E, F-sharp, G, are later changed at m. 17 to E, E, F-sharp, G-sharp.

Rhythm

Except for several meter changes of one measure's duration, which are not very significant, the meter is regular 3/4 time and the note values are almost exclusively quarters and eighths. However, in the climactic section which begins at m. 17, there are measures of quadruple meter as well as running 16th notes. The longest sixteenth-note run occurs just before the return of the opening material at m. 33. There is syncopation in the bass part at m. 17 which contrasts with the regular eighth-note accompaniment pattern.

There are also several *accelerando* and *a tempo* markings, but they usually last for only one measure.

Melody

The melody of this movement is the soprano note of a series of chords, with the melodic line moving in a step-wise direction. There are more than enough indications which instruct the player to project the music in a vocal style. The flowing, arpeggiated bass creates the effect of a nocturne. When Ben-Haim wishes to get more intense, he often changes to a higher or lower register. At m. 9 he has the same melody singing an octave higher than the opening and the four-note chord now has five notes. At m. 33 the return of the opening material is cast an octave lower than the beginning. He also starts the middle section at m. 17 in the middle register, and when the intensity increases at m. 25 he states a similar melody an octave higher. The piece has a regular four-bar phrase structure throughout.

Structural Level

Clarity

Ben-Haim abandons the broken-chord accompaniment at the beginning of the second section, which sets it apart from the first. The return of this section at m. 33 is marked by the resumption of the same broken-chord pattern, but only for that one measure. After that point, a variant is used as the accompaniment and this gradually comes to dominate the music until the end.

Proportion

This piece is quite symmetrical in design with the opening statement being an exact double period of sixteen measures, the second portion, which is a variation of the first, is again a double period of sixteen measures. The final statement starting at m. 33

and continuing on to the end is twelve measures. The main climax occurs a little more than half way through.

There are a total of forty-four measures and the climax begins at m. 25.

Each return of the main theme at mm. 17 and 33. is like a memory of what came before. This effect is heightened by the dynamic markings, pianissimo and amoroso at m. 17, and *pianissimo, quasi lontano* at m. 33.

Integrity

Unity is achieved throughout this piece through the use of step-wise, chordal melodic passages and arpeggiated basses. In the contrasting section at m. 17 we still have the step-wise melody, this time in a more austere form with single notes instead of chords and a syncopated bass, derived from what came before.

The rhythm has running 16th-notes which are improvisationa in character. The dynamic level rises and the left hand uses syncopation which is smooth and subtle and skillfully prepares the climatic point at m. 25.

Complexity

The piece does not contain much contrasting material. For instance, the middle section is essentially a variation of the opening material. The texture is thinner and the melodic writing contains more embellishment. This work comes between two fiery movements and provides a point of lyrical repose.

Subtlety

A motif which occurs toward the end of the work at m. 34,

Example 4, *Canzonetta*, m. 34

grows directly out of the first three notes in the soprano:

Example 5. *Canzonetta*, m. 1.

The tenor part, A-B, is derived from the rising opening chords. This little motif becomes an insistent calling suddenly heard in mm. 34, 36, 38, 40 and 41. These notes create a poignant statement which has not been heard earlier in this movement.

Because of the music's subdued nature, Ben-Haim rarely provides the listener with sharp contrasts. When he deviates from the conventional and becomes unpredictable, the result is often quietly intense, growing out of what had come before and provides one with a different kind of "shock value" than through loud outbursts.

Toccata

Stylistic Level

Sonority

A toccata is defined in the *Harvard Dictionary* as an important type of early keyboard music originating in the sixteenth century and cultivated mainly during the Baroque period. Its chief characteristic is the combination of various styles, improvisatory, virtuoso, fugal, etc; the whole being designed to exploit the resources of the instrument as well as the ingenuity of the composer and the virtuosity of the performer.

Although most of this piece is at a subdued dynamic level, there is a tremendous intensity and driving force from the very beginning to the very end. The first forte isn't heard until m. 101, and this is modified by *forte/piano* markings at mm. 112, 114, etc. The first real climax arrives at m. 167 and this is built up to gradually from m. 135, where Ben-Haim indicates, *crescendo poco a poco*. The main climax is at m. 191, marked *fortississimo*. The power of the climactic ending is augmented by the use of alternating octaves and chords instead of single notes with which the piece began.

Harmony

This piece is clearly in the key of E minor until m. 119, where there is a lyrical and improvisatory melody in the key of C-sharp minor. The piece modulates through various keys until it ends in the original E minor. At m. 51 there is a more contrapuntal section, consisting of eighth-notes in the bass and chromatic sixteenths in the right hand. At the requisite speed and in the deep bass this produces a blurring effect on the piano. There is a reiteration of the beginning at m. 70, with the opening motif in octaves. The tied chords at mm. 185, 187 and 189 are an expansion the three intervals of a third found at m. 47.

Rhythm

As in most toccatas, the rhythm is regular and propulsive. The first break in this regularity is at m. 51 with the introduction of an eighth rest on the first beat, giving the piece added rhythmical excitement. Just before the improvisatory section at m. 119 there is a series of meter changes which tends to break up the predictability of the meter's regularity.

There are several places where small ritards are in order from a musical point of view. The first is at m. 118 and precedes a new section, while the second is m. 166 and ends a major section.

Melody

The technical device of alternating hands which pervades this movement produces a hidden melody. The beginning has such an example:

Example 6. *Toccata*, m. 2.

The eighth-note figure produced by 16ths in m. 2 is more fully realized at m. 147 where it appears as parallel sevenths and later at m. 158 in octaves.

M. 119 is the only instance where there is true contrasting melodic material. It recalls a Middle Eastern, melismatic, quarter tone chant. It is lyrical as opposed to the percussive, driving repeated notes that have dominated the piece up to now. The left hand part is a clear statement of the theme in varied form which at the opening of the movement was only implied. At m. 119 there are two separate melodies juxtaposed.

Although the melody begins simply with its repeated E's, it expands to the use of octaves in the left hand at m. 70 in a lower register. Its final statement is projected, first in fragmented form from m. 158-191, and then in its full glory at m. 192, marked *con tutta forza* with "blind" octaves played as fast as possible in a higher register. This provides an appropriately brilliant, *martellato* ending to the movement.

Structural Level

Clarity

The alternating sixteenths which are typical of most modern toccatas are dominated by fifty measures of repeated E's. The tension this formula generates is finally relieved at m. 51, where a new pattern is established. Here, Ben-Haim still uses sixteenths, but with a chromatically evolved melodic line which is in sharp contrast to the previous section. This chromatic idea is further exploited and developed beginning at m 123.

Respite from the headlong propulsion of sixteenths is finally provided by eighth notes starting at m. 145.

Proportion

This piece is made up of several sections of various lengths. The technical device of alternating repeated notes used at the beginning governs the entire work, with a few exceptions such as mm. 51 and 119. A little more than halfway through the piece (m.

119) there is completely new section, which is developed until the return of the original material in greatly augmented form at m. 192.

Although this piece has the most number of pages, its presto tempo makes it speed by in less time than many of the shorter movements.

Integrity

The entire work is integrated through the use of repeated notes alternating between the hands. The next important unifying idea occurs at m. 119 which is based on the new rhythmical material introduced at m. 51. The concinnity of the elements is coordinated through the use of melody (repeated notes, alternating hands), rhythm (regularity of meter, interspersed with a few meter changes), and harmony (alternating consonant and dissonant sections, with the tonality rooted in E minor). All these elements work together to produce a piece of brilliance and fire.

Complexity

This piece is made up of two themes which are developed and expanded upon, moving from statements of delicate transparency and simplicity to thick-textured, *martellato* passages. The primary and secondary themes are strongly contrasting; the opening melody is percussive and diatonic, while the second theme (m. 119) is more lyrical and legato.

Texturally Ben-Haim structures this music so that the opening is lighter and thinner while from the second theme on the texture becomes thicker and more complex.

Subtlety

A device utilized by Ben-Haim and employed to intensify the excitement of certain sections is the use of tied half-notes against the sixteenth-note movement at mm. 67 through 78. Toward the end of the piece, mm. 168-172, this pedal point device is augmented by the use of octaves and chords.

One passage that is out of character with the rest of the piece is mm. 51-58, with its highly chromatic movement and low registration. When played at the requisite speed, this passage sounds vague and blurred. Compared to the rest of this work, the Toccata stands alone in its frank appeal to virtuoso brilliance.

Notes

1. Paul Ben-Haim, Biographical Pamphlet. (Tel Aviv, 1967).

FIVE PIECES FOR PIANO
Paul Ben-Haim, Op 34, 1943

PASTORALE

CANZONETTA

Chapter Three

CAPRICCIO AGITATO

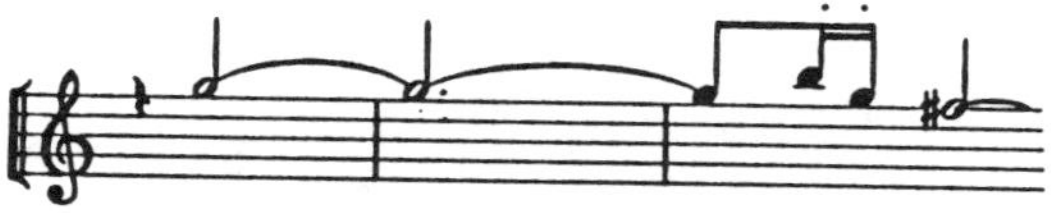

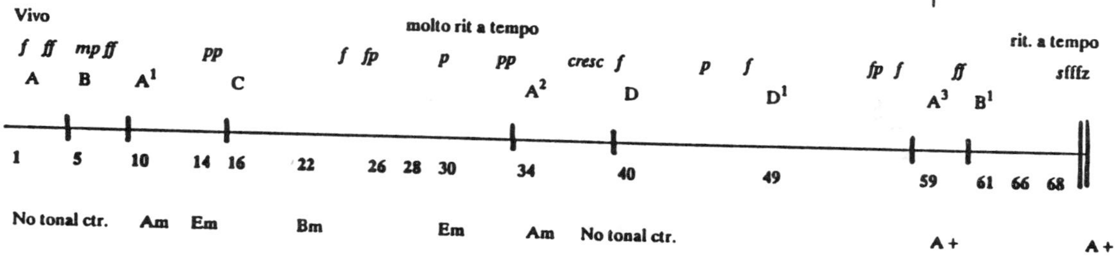

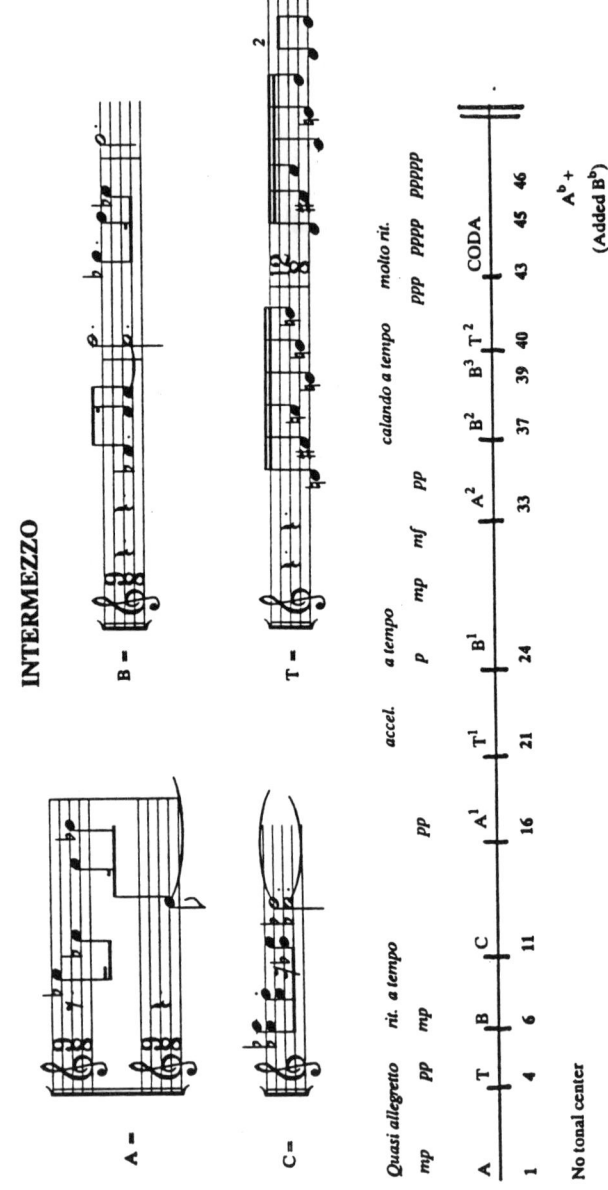

Chapter Three

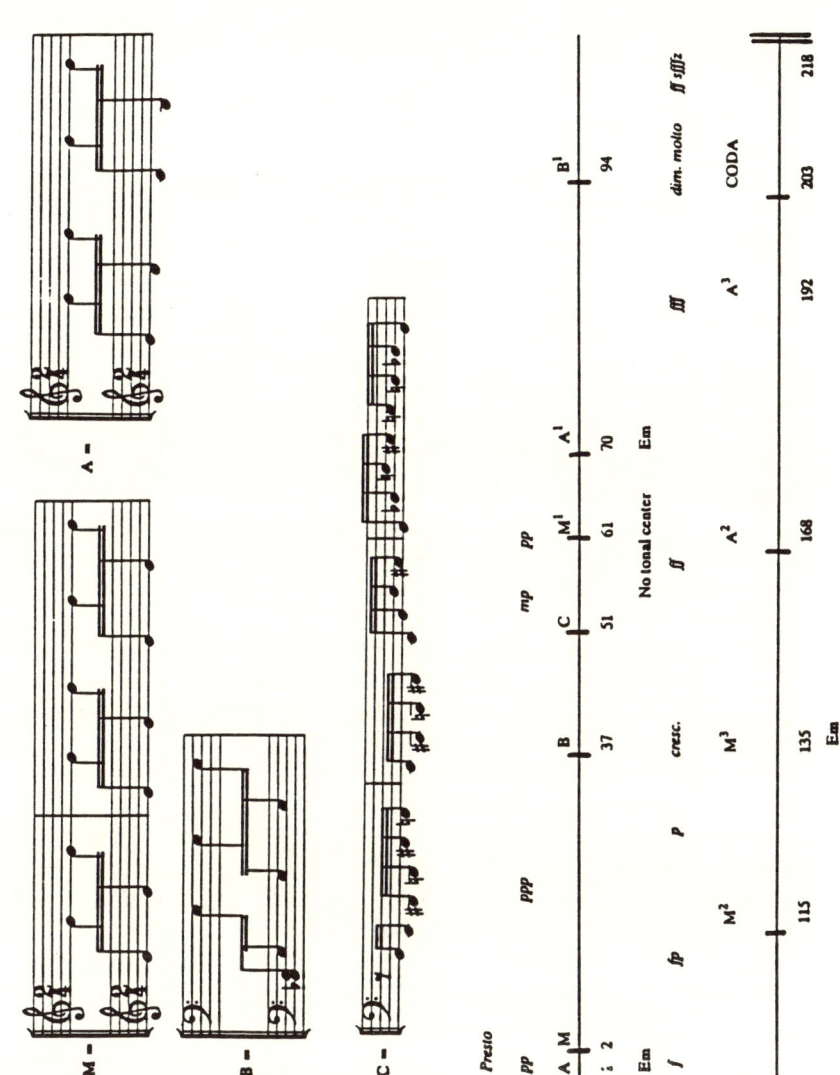

Chapter Four

MELODY AND VARIATIONS

1950

Of the origin of the theme of these variations, Ben-Haim has written:

> I composed the melody (without variations) as a little piano piece for children—or beginners—as commissioned by Mr. Moshe Gorali for the "Davar Children's Weekly;" the piece, as it appeared in the paper was similar in form and character to the first variation of the present work. As I played it over time and again it occurred to me that the melody lent itself well to further elaboration and I decided to use it for a set of variations for young pianists: the theme was greatly simplified (the melody being presented in unison and in octaves) and the original piece became the first variation, which in turn inspired new variations. Yet while at work on the elaboration of my original material, I felt that there was a considerable force of expression latent in the seemingly unassuming melody—just as closer acquaintance of people often makes one detect qualities that one would hardly suspect in them at a first casual meeting. Intimate acquaintance with my own little melody made me change the tone of my work the eighth variation: it suddenly assumed an almost menacing strain and then became in turn passionate, affectionate, meditative—losing its erstwhile youthful character completely.[1]

Although the *Theme* is seemingly simple and child-like, it is the product of a highly sophisticated musical mind. It very simplicity and feeling of incompleteness lends itself to further elaboration.

The Theme and each variation of this work will be analyzed as a whole, since, unlike the *Variations on a Hebrew Melody*, it is much shorter and its variations are more integrated.

Chapter Three

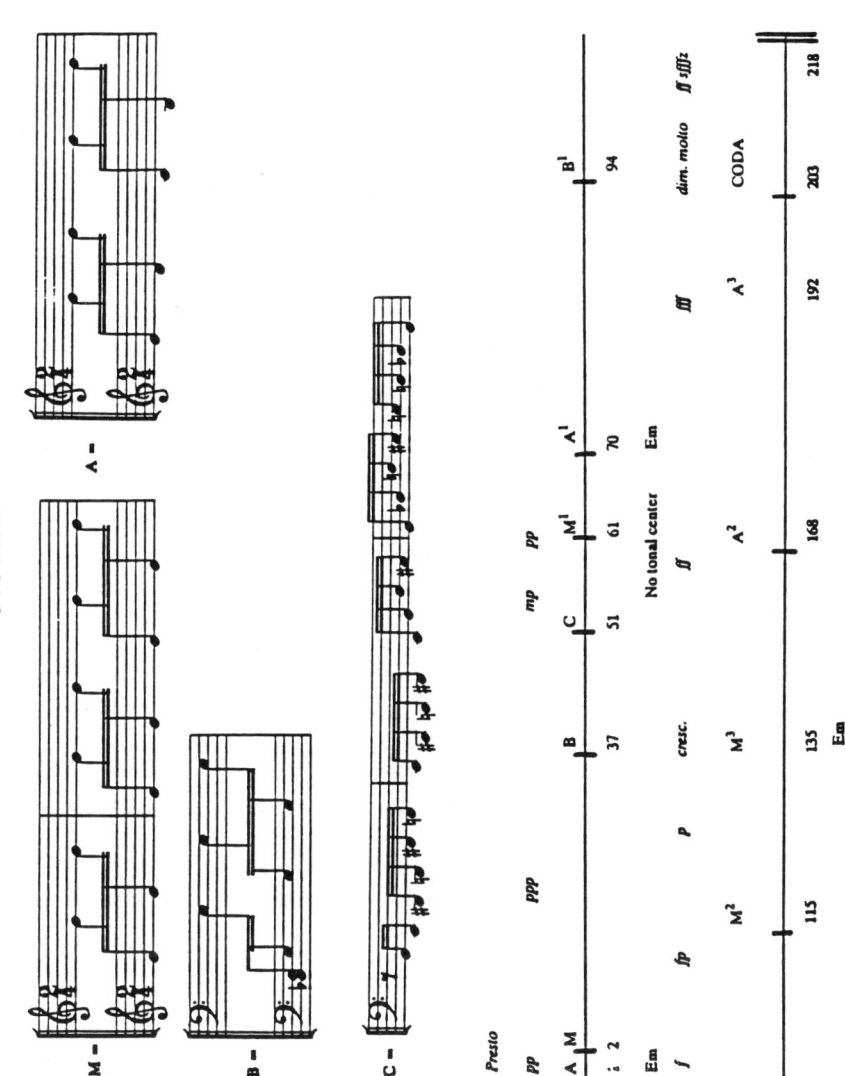

Chapter Four

MELODY AND VARIATIONS

1950

Of the origin of the theme of these variations, Ben-Haim has written:

> I composed the melody (without variations) as a little piano piece for children — or beginners — as commissioned by Mr. Moshe Gorali for the "Davar Children's Weekly;" the piece, as it appeared in the paper was similar in form and character to the first variation of the present work. As I played it over time and again it occurred to me that the melody lent itself well to further elaboration and I decided to use it for a set of variations for young pianists: the theme was greatly simplified (the melody being presented in unison and in octaves) and the original piece became the first variation, which in turn inspired new variations. Yet while at work on the elaboration of my original material, I felt that there was a considerable force of expression latent in the seemingly unassuming melody — just as closer acquaintance of people often makes one detect qualities that one would hardly suspect in them at a first casual meeting. Intimate acquaintance with my own little melody made me change the tone of my work the eighth variation: it suddenly assumed an almost menacing strain and then became in turn passionate, affectionate, meditative — losing its erstwhile youthful character completely.[1]

Although the *Theme* is seemingly simple and child-like, it is the product of a highly sophisticated musical mind. It very simplicity and feeling of incompleteness lends itself to further elaboration.

The Theme and each variation of this work will be analyzed as a whole, since, unlike the *Variations on a Hebrew Melody*, it is much shorter and its variations are more integrated.

Calmo e senza espressione

Stylistic level

Sonority

The dynamic range of the entire piece is from *pppp* to *ff*, although the prevailing dynamic is often *piano* or softer. There are three instances where the music builds to *fortissimo*. The first one starts at m. 97 marked *forte subito* and continues to m. 114, which is marked *fortissimo*, the next at m. 119, marked, *sffz* and finally at m. 210. These places denote the climaxes of this work and close observation shows that the writing also gets denser there.

The wide range of the piano is exploited in this work. In each climactic section, mm. 97, 114 and 210, the distance between the two hands becomes farther apart, producing a decidedly dramatic effect. At m. 210 the directions are *molto vivo ed appassianato*.

Harmony

The opening of the piece states the theme, *Calmo e senza espressione* in unison in the dorian mode. In fact, the music remains that mode until the fifth variation which begins to show bi-tonality, starting in C sharp minor and ending in D sharp minor. The sixth variation begins suggesting C major and ends in E minor with an added C-sharp. The next, *Allegretto grazzioso* starts in what could be F major and ends in D, but whether major or minor cannot be determined. In Variation 8, Ben-Haim returns to dorian mode with a pedal point on D at mm. 148-150. The listener is then thrown off with the A and B in the bass leading to Variation 9, which doesn't start out with a clear tonality but ends in dorian mode. Variation 10 has a very unclear tonality, suggesting E-flat, but this key is neverthe less obscured because of the omission of A-Flat. Variation 11 is in D major and 12 seems to hover around D major but ends reiterating the note F sharp. The last variation ends in D major. This piece has a mix of tonal and modal-harmonic sections, with each variation taking on its own character, largely as a result of its harmony and design.

Rhythm

The meter of this piece is mostly in 4/4 or 2/4 time except for several instances where it changes to 5/4 or 7/8. Those instances, however, are significant. It is first at Variation 4 that a 5/4 meter is encountered, and the melodic line is very florid and melismatic in its realization. The 5/4 and 7/8 meters are often used in Middle-Eastern-sounding melodies, which enhance their exotic consequence. The 7/8 meter is found in the penultimate variation, number 12, and is used to bring out the brilliant effect required of this section, marked *molto vivo ed appassionato.*

There are also several instances of change of meter, with a particularly curious one occurring at Variation 7, starting at m. 133, where the meter goes from 6/4 to 7/4 to 4/4. Although the meter is common time in the ninth variation, the writing style is very different from anything that came before, with slow single whole notes, a type of unfolding, cello-like melody. Ben-Haim does start with 4/4 meter and ends the same way. There is also a syncopated 7/4 meter in Variation 7 which gives the music a dancing, lilting quality. Therefore as the music gets more florid and expressive, the meters become more exotic

Melody

The melody at the opening is very straightforward, simple and clear. It is repetitious in the manner of children's music and repeats three times with the consequent melody also repeating three times. The mordents serve an important function by bringing out the long quarter notes and implying a Middle Eastern ornament. The first variation is more chordal and more notes are added to the melody; it is a clear continuation of what came before.

Variation 2 is in the style of a nocturne, with an arpeggiated bass and a lyrical melody in the right hand.

Variation 3 is like a toccata making the melody into quick, short staccato notes.

Variation 4, with its 5/4 meter is ornate, melismatic and has an improvisatory character, with a very simple chordal bass.

Variation 5 has a much more spaced out melody, leaping from bass to treble, recalling a *hora* rhythm which is eventually reinforced with parallel fifths and fourths.

The 6th variation is almost a humorous setting with the original melody turned upside down, single notes in the bass and chords in the upper register. Yet there is an underlying energy and sense of forward propulsion. Variation 7 turns to octaves and syncopa- tion in the right hand and open fifths in the bass and a 7/4 meter.

Variation 8 has an improvisatory flute or bird-like melody with rolled chords in the bass.

Variation 9 is very mysterious with lower register notes in the bass and right hand, which gradually unfolds into a toccata.

The 10th variation is similar to the last movement of the Sonatina and has a forward-moving propulsion and a directness of purpose.

The 11th variation changes mood dramatically, to one of seriousness and reflection. It is much more homophonic that some of the other sections.

The 12th requires a brilliant sound, with the octaves in the right hand and the 16th runs in the bass and its strong dynamics.

Variation 13 reverts to a reflective type of mood and also uses the opening notes in a different position. As is Ben-Haim's habit there is his very special brand of unison writing, representing poignant nostalgia and recalling the opening measures of this piece.

Structural Level

Clarity

Although there are 13 variations in this work, Ben-Haim has not numbered them as is customary. This is significant, since almost all the variations run into each other without a break, and the piece as a whole is more integrated than most sets of variations. However, they are set apart from one another with many different tempi and meter signatures.

In the second movement of his piano sonata Op. 111, Beethoven also omitted variation numbers, and that movement is also highly integrated and played without breaks. This comment is by no means meant to compare Beethoven's work with Ben-Haim's. It is simply an intriguing observation, especially in light of the fact that the composer was known to have publicly performed Op. 111.

Proportion

The proportions of this work are almost classical in their balance and symmetry. The theme and the first eight variations are built on either eight or sixteen measure phrase structures. Variation 8 deviates slightly, having fourteen measures, and number 9 nearly doubles this with 26. Then Variation 10 and 11 return to the sixteen bar format and the piece ends with two variations of twenty-three measures each. One wonders whether Ben-Haim's Germanic training might account for this strict observance of symmetrical phrase structure.

Integrity

Because this work is a set of variations on a theme, it is obvious that its unity derives from each variation's relationship to the theme. On closer examination, for example, one sees that the rising and falling sequence which comprises the theme's first measure is reiterated in sometimes different guises in the succeeding variations.

The theme and the last variation are both written with a unison melody as a binding device, which is an important stylistic element of Ben-Haim's writing in general.

Complexity

As a whole, this work is simple and straightforward in structure and style. The theme upon which it is based is childlike and unpretentious. However, certain variations (No. 7, 12, and 13 for instance), are much more complex and require a mature and sophisticated musicianship.

Subtlety

In the beginning, this piece establishes a predictable pattern in its consistent use of eight or sixteen measure lengths, and its lightness of spirit.

However, in terms and strangeness and avoidance of predictability, Variation 9 is different from all the rest. It is in a lower register, and begins with slow, cello-like whole-notes. The use of the damper pedal through the first 8 measures, creates a mysterious impressionistic sonority.

Notes

1. Paul Ben-Haim, preface to 1953 edition of "Melody andVariations," (Tel Aviv: Israeli Music Publications, 1953)

The Music of Paul Ben-Haim

Melody and Variations
Paul Ben-Haim, 1950

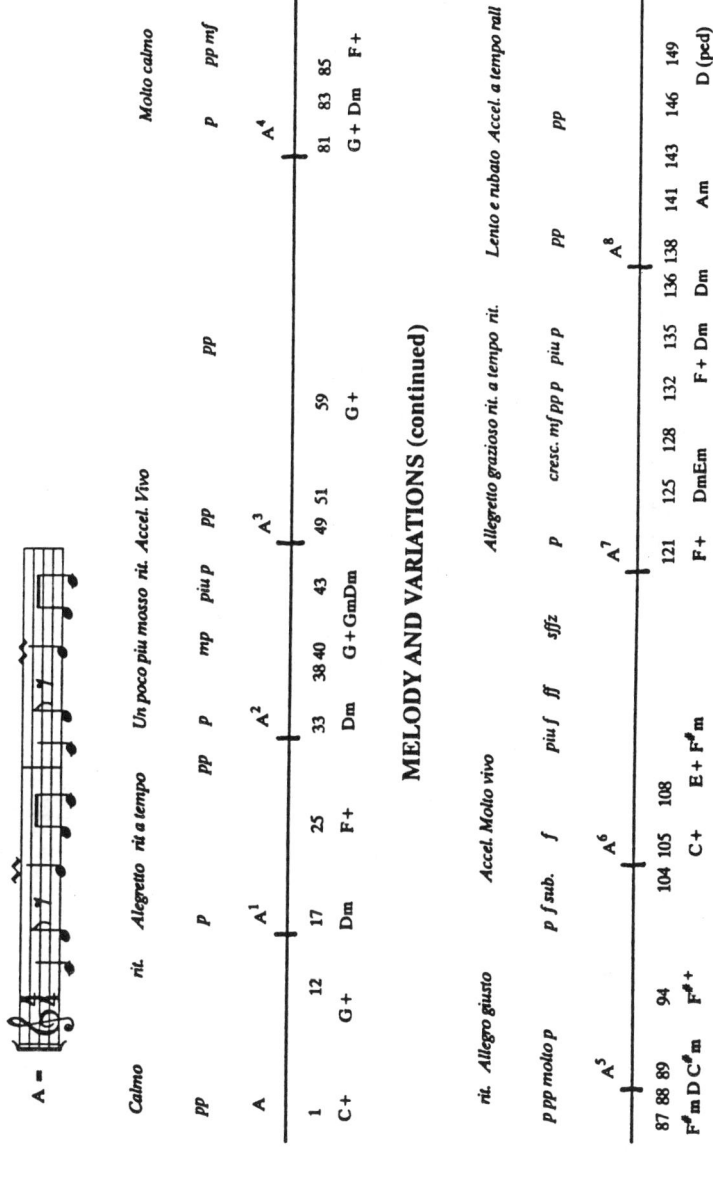

74   Chapter Four

Melody and Variations (continued)

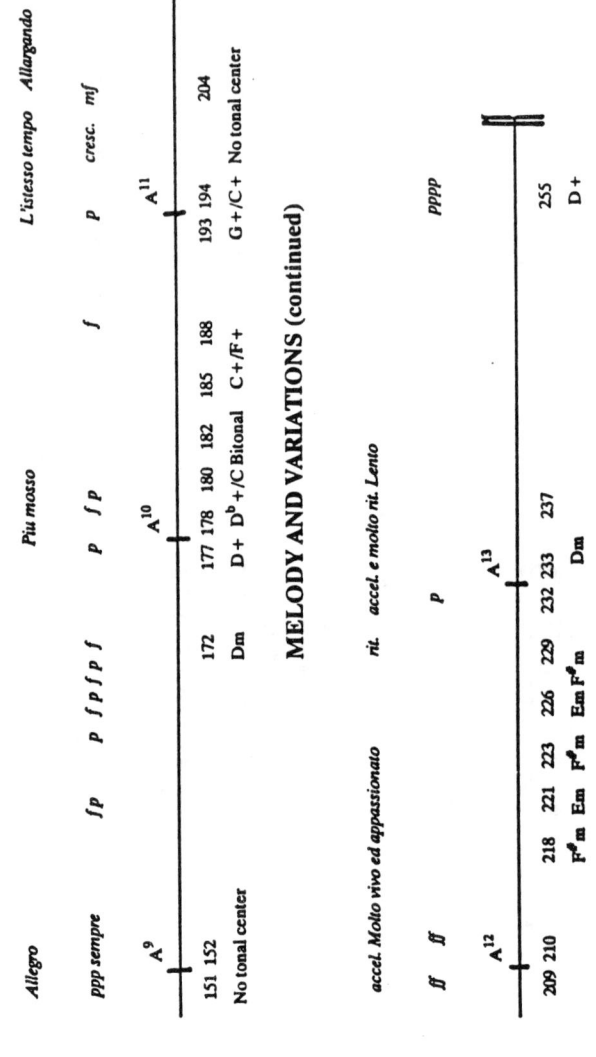

Chapter Five

THREE SONGS WITHOUT WORDS

Ben-Haim conceived his "Three Songs Without Words" as vocalises for high voice and piano but it later occurred to him that "Songs" lent themselves as well to instrumental performance; the various versions for solo instrument and piano are the composer's own arrangements of the vocalises.[1]

The composer explains the three parts of this little Suite as "tone pictures of an oriental mood" and adds that:

> Whoever's imagination needs additional prompting may think that the long-breathed melodies of the Arioso were inspired by the mood of a summer day's pitiless heat in the bare Judean Hills. The Ballad pictures the monotonous babbling of an Oriental story-teller, while the last song is based on a traditional folk tune of Sephardic-Jewish origin — a veritable pearl which I have only given a setting.[2]

Arioso

Stylistic Level

Sonority

As in many of Ben-Haim's works, the opening from mm. 1 to 15 is marked *pianissimo*. Moreover, the first measure is marked *sordino* indicating the use of the una corda pedal in the piano part. Dolce e cantabile in the solo part suggests that Ben-Haim conceived these pieces as songs as much as instrumental works. It is at m. 16 that the word *crescendo* appears in the piano part and in the following measure, mezzo forte is indicated, then back to piano. It is the crescendo starting at m. 34 which leads to the major climax of the piece at m. 40. This is followed by a return to the original idea with a much simpler and starker accompaniment. The word *indifferente* over the viola's part (m. 42), is related to Ben-Haim's statement, "An instrumentalist playing the Three Songs should renounce all tendencies of virtuoso brilliance in favor of a purely melodic expression."[2] Thus the performer should avoid all excess emotion and declamation and simply play the notes as written.

The dissonant opening chords in the piano, which are like tone clusters conflict with the dreamy, pastoral instrumental melody. Ben-Haim often does something similar: a quasi-peaceful melody juxtaposed with an ambiguous and tension-filled harmony.

Harmony

This piece is clearly in the key of C major. However our sense of tonality is somewhat jarred by the inclusion of the B-natural with the C octaves. After m. 4 the harmonic rhythm gets faster with changes every measure until m. 11. Although the opening implies the key of C major, the voice part suggests A minor, but without any clear-cut establishment of that tonality.

The next significant harmonic change is at m. 22 where C-sharp dominates, making an enharmonic change to D-flat at m. 30. Finally, at m. 35, F alternates with D-flat (C-sharp) for prominence, and this eventually brings the harmony back to an unambiguous C at m. 41.

Rhythm

The meter of this movement is largely unchanged except for several places where it shifts from triple to quadruple, mm. 17 and 21. Both spots are intended to extend the florid melodic line. The use of 3/2 meter indicates that the composer wanted a broader melodic line, with a less intrusive bar-line.

The use of dotted quarters and rests in the accompaniment throughout the movement contrasts strikingly with the sensuous, legato melody above and creates a suspenseful mood. Except for the *molto moderato* marking in the opening, there are no other written-in tempo changes except for a fermata sign with *"breve"* over it at m. 40, which immediately precedes the return of the opening material.

An important feature of the rhythmic scheme is the use of a quarter rest preceding the opening melody, which gives the piece a feeling of forward movement. This device is used quite consistently throughout the piece.

Melody

This movement consists of one melody with variations; the melody being the opening step-wise pattern of quarter-notes followed by 8th-notes, resolving into a dotted-quarter. The opening is diatonic and in the key of A minor. Every time the main melody appears, at mm. 2, 5, 30 and 42, it is always in the same register and has the character of a melisma or vocalise. Indeed, a vocalise was what these pieces were meant to be.

At m. 12 a new theme is introduced consisting of skips of thirds, fourths and fifths and continuing with new rhythmic patterns.

At m. 30, there is a significant alteration to the main theme: the B becomes B-flat, and the D becomes D-flat and the G from m. 3 becomes G-flat, producing a very oriental-sounding augmented second. This effect is altered again at m. 43 where the half-note is back to G- natural.

Structural Level

Clarity

The most striking accompaniment device in this work is the insistent repeated chord formula, articulated by rests. This pattern is found throughout the movement, except for the last two measures.

Another unifying element is the five quarters and four 8th notes first heard in m. 2. It is later transposed down a half-step and displaced rhythmically by three beats, starting on the count of four instead of two. Its return appearance at m. 30 is further modified by changing B to B-flat and D to D-flat.

Proportion

This piece is very symmetrically proportioned. There are 52 measures and exactly half way through at m. 26 is the middle section discussed above, which is a variant of the opening melody, but in C-sharp minor.

The first 24 measures contain the opening statement, then the next 16 measures include the next important statement, and the last 12 measures, the final one. Proportionally the movement is structured into 12 and 12, 16, and then 12 again.

The climax occurs more than half way through the work, starting at m. 35. This climax is also important structurally because it ends an entire section and immediately precedes the return of the original statement.

Integrity

This movement is unified through the use of the step-wise descending and ascending melody with which it opens. Also, the insistent, though subdued accompaniment with its triple meter and 8th-note rests is an element which is used consistently throughout the movement.

Because there is one melody, the opening is the basis for everything else that happens. At m. 12 it is varied through the use of larger intervals. At the C-sharp minor section at m. 26, it is modified through the use of a key change. It forms the basis for transition and development (m. 26), as well as the return in the final statement.

In terms of concinnity, all the musical elements adhere to an economy of design and are interrelated.

Complexity

Contrasts in this piece mainly occur in the way of subtle harmonic, rhythmic and melodic changes. Sometimes the composer will stay with one harmony for an extended period, such as the chords in the first three measures, and then in the left hand simply change one note — the C to a D and add two notes in right hand.

Rhythmically what was a quarter going to a dotted half note, (m. 15), becomes an 8th going to a dotted quarter in m. 17, and finally a dotted 8th and a 16th. This results in a rhythmic foreshortening which adds intensity to the melodic line.

Since this piece is based on one theme, it is important to observe how Ben-Haim develops it. This is done by spacing the notes further apart, changing tonality and the use of embellishments.

Textures in the opening 24 measures are pinner than in the middle of the piece. An inner voice which is only hinted at in m. 3, is more extensively developed at m. 23. At the modified return of the original theme at m. 42 the accompaniment textures are as sparse as possible.

Subtlety

Through Ben-Haim's constant use of repeated chords in triple meter, might seem far from subtle, but on closer observation, it becomes apparent that this perpetual motion device becomes an integral part of the entire musical idea and is directly related to the work's musical meaning. This music has features derived from skill and subtlety within its confines, and results in a structurally clear and concise design.

Two noteworthy points are the grace notes in m. 41, making a variant of the opening accompaniment formula, and the last note, G, which adds to the ambiguity of the harmony. Another is the addition of an imitation of the opening 8th-note melody in the piano part at m. 24, and further on at m. 32.

Ballad

Stylistic Level

Sonority

The *Harvard Dictionary of Music* defines "Ballad" as ". . . a popular song, usually combining romantic and narrative, often adventurous elements." The "narrative" portion of the "Ballad" is the opening, measures 1 through 16. This is an insistent, sing-song chant-like figure, calling to mind an ancient story teller. At 17 the "romantic" portion starts.

Often in this piece, a dynamic climax occurs where one of the other parts drops out. First there is a *forte* at m. 45 where the piano is silent. Next at m. 160 where there is no viola part, and the last one is at m. 85 where the piano drops out again.

The movement begins *piano* and maintains that effect until the first statement ends at m. 16. There are some *mezzo fortes*, mainly in the second section at m. 17 and 39. At 17, the solo part is set off against an impressionistic blur created by playing the D-flat scale with the pedal held down.

The main climax of the piece occurs at m. 94, marked "*sffz*" It is also here that the texture of the piano accompaniment is thickest.

Harmony

The piece is clearly in F minor and Oriental in sound with its close intervals and frequent melodic embellishments. Not only is F minor introduced, but is established strongly because of its constant repetition.

The frequent embellished melodies of 16th notes as in m. 31 against 8th notes in the solo part are contrapuntal in texture and especially at the very end which has imitative counterpoint at m. 118. Although there are three voices, the top part often doubles the treble piano part.

Rhythm

Except for one instance of a meter change, the rhythm is a regular 2/4 time throughout the movement. Rhythmically, the piece is built on the following pattern: an 8th rest and then three 8th notes, repeated three times, then four 16th and two 8ths.

Example 7. *Ballad*, m. 1-4

A more legato section starting at m. 17 is rhythmically more expansive with longer notes than the opening. At mm. 45-46 the notes get still longer with half notes in the melody. Because this piece is so rhythmically active, places such as mm. 45 and 57 stand out because there is a sudden halt to the motion, the piano drops out and the soloist's long notes prevail and contrast sharply with the previous rhythmic activity.

The opening is marked *Allegretto* and the next significant tempo change, *Rubato (senza tempo)* is at m. 94 which implies an improvisatory style. This lasts until the a tempo at m. 101. Then there is a broadening of the tempo at m. 118 *un poco meno mosso* which lasts until the end of the movement. This broadening expands through *Ritardando* to *Lento*.

Melody

The melody of this work creates a combination of Oriental sounds, with touches of impressionistic color. It is organized in a pattern related to the original definition of a Ballad. The first 16 measures being musical narrative or dialogue, while starting at m. 17, the second part is the romantic element: more legato, broader, longer lines and in direct contrast to what came before. Then the monotony of the Oriental storyteller returns at m. 25.

The piece goes from narrative to romantic themes throughout, following each other and becoming more embellished until the end where they become transparent again.

In general, the melodies are in the same register except for two notable spots: the climax, starting in the solo part at m. 45, and the rubato part at m. 94. The highest register of the piano occurs at its climax starting at m. 69. So it is clear that the composer aims for a higher register at climactic moments in this work.

The direction, *indifferente e quasi raccontando* defines the way this melody is to be interpreted; in a monotonous manner reminiscent of an Oriental storyteller.

Structural Level

Clarity

The most striking aspect of this movement is its use of repeated motifs, both in the piano accompaniment and in the solo part.

m. 1.   m. 31

m. 18-19

Example 8. *Ballad*, mm. 1, 18-19, 31.

Although this is a separate movement, it resembles the Arioso in its use of these ostinato devices which form a unifying element for the entire movement. There is also an impressionistic effect in the piano part which Ben-Haim uses as a cadential device or to introduce a new idea. This effect is found at mm. 13-16, 67- 69, and 114-117.

Proportion

This work has 131 measures and near the middle (m. 70) is the main climax, a piano solo marked *forte* and *giocoso*. The other climax occurs at m. 93 and is in the solo part against a long-held chord in the piano.

The opening statement is 16 measures long; the "romantic" statement is 8 measures long. The next phrase starting at m. 25 is 32 measures in length. These are all multiples of 8. The next phrase, starting at m. 59 is again 8 measures long.

The climaxes are skillfully prepared, both architecturally and musically. Every major phrase is either 8 or 16 measures, except for the last one, starting at m. 108, which is 14 measures long. It is important to note that although the phrases look short and fragmented, they are part of a much larger design. Dynamic climaxes also adhere to the symmetrical proportion.

Integrity

This piece is unified through the use of two contrasting themes, the opening consisting of short, repeated fragments and the second theme, starting at m. 17, with its expansive, song-like sonority. Also the opening has much smaller intervals, reminiscent of an Oriental sound, and the "romantic" portion has larger intervals, more expansive and emotional in character. These two themes form the basis for all rhythmic, harmonic and melodic development.

The most obvious example of how Ben-Haim integrates this music is through rhythmic and harmonic interaction. The concinnity of the elements is also related through the use of repetitive rhythmic patterns. The melody, also repetitive and quite Oriental in color, is balanced by the simpler, underlying harmony which is quite obviously in the key of F minor. All this comes together to call to mind the picture of a overly verbose storyteller.

Complexity

The primary and secondary themes present a strong contrast to each other. The former is largely fragmented, repetitive and is conjunct intervalically; the latter (m. 17) is more expressive, lyrical, and is less repetitive. The first theme's structure implies a non-expressive interpretation which is indicated by the word *indifferente*. The second theme could be played slightly slower, as suggested by the word *espressivo*, especially since the piano has virtually dropped out at this point.

Textures in the beginning are quite transparent due to the use of unison melodies between the piano and solo parts, while at m. 37 the texture becomes more dense, yet still quite linear. The four measures start ing m. 74 are definitely more polyphonic. Beginning at m. 118 there is an episode of imitative counterpoint, but is not elaborated upon.

Although Ben-Haim only presents two themes, he develops them to their fullest potential and creates musical ideas of complexity and simplicity.

Subtlety

The word *raccontando* relates directly to the programmatic content of "Ballad" and is reflected in the fragmented, repeated motifs, which are to be performed in a non-expressive manner. An avoidance of expectations occurs whenever the composer interjects the two long half-notes, (mm.45-46, 57-58) creating a suspension of forward movement and interrupting the regularly recurring patterns. The piano accompaniment also drops out at these points. Another hiatus is created by the impressionistic pedal effects at mm. 13, 94 and 114.

Sephardic Melody

Stylistic Level

Sonority

Unlike most of Ben-Haim's works, the dynamic level dominating this piece is *forte* and sometimes *fortissimo*. The tempo and expression marks opening the work, *Largamente, rubato e molto appassionato*, indicate a striking contrast to the subdued intensity of the previous movements. There are several climactic points, the first being an instrumental interlude marked *fortissimo* starting at m. 18, which precedes the return of the main theme at m. 22. The main climax is at m. 24 where the writing is densest, and the piano part doubles the melody in octaves. Another powerful place is mm. 33-36 which begins *forte* and ends *fortissimo*. Then there is a sudden change from *fortissimo* to *ppp* at mm. 36-41. Another point of extreme intensity is the continuation of *ppp* to the end of the movement.

At the two loudest points mm. 22 and 36, the register is also higher than it has been so far, thus enhancing the emotional energy of the passage. In contrast to the general density of the texture, the beginning and ending represent a striking difference in sonority, being sparsely written and rhapsodic in style.

Harmony

This piece begins in the key of E minor, but meanders through several ambiguous tonalities, never clearly establishing a home key. The opening measure where the piano enters with an F-sharp is an example of this ambiguity; the expected E is delayed until the next measure. The last three measures also tend to confuse the listener; m. 46 is clearly in E minor but the following two measures seem to veer off toward B minor, the dominant minor. This delaying of the expected harmony by several measures adds a touch of tension and dissonance to the piece.

Rhythm

Largamente rubato e molto appassionato is suggestive of the fiery and impassioned character of this movement. The 3/4 meter is unchanged except for several place where it shifts from triple to quadruple time, but only for one measure; for example mm. 23, 29 and 33. However, the pulse changes considerably with written in tempo changes occurring at significant structural points, such as m. 15, marked *Molto mosso,* m. 22, marked *Largamente come prima, mosso* at m. 36, and finally *Largo* at m. 41. It is at m. 15 where the intensity of the work increases and then changes back to *Largamente* at the return of the opening theme at m. 22. The entire rhythmic structure of the piece is freer, more rhapsodic and improvisatory than the two which precede it.

Melody

The most important feature of the melody is the closeness of the intervals and the use of the augmented 2nd, giving it an undeniable Middle Eastern flavor. Also the very first note with its fermata already shows a strong, declamatory character. The fact that there are three fermatas in the irregular opening five-bar phrase also reinforces the improvisatory character of the movement. As the intensity of the work increases, so too do the melodic skips; at m. 9 there is the upward skip of a 4th, at m. 11, a 6th, and at m. 13, an 11th.

While the opening and closing portions of the movement consist of odd-numbered phrases, the middle section, beginning at m. 21 has four-bar phrasing. However, because of the fanciful accompaniment, there is still an element of improvisation. The entire movement can be considered one long-lined, continuous melody.

Structural Level

Clarity

In contrast to the two movements which preceded it, this work is improvisatory in style. Its tempo indication reads *Largamente rubato e molto appassionato* and throughout the work, there are many tempo changes, fermatas and a wide variety of rhythmic subdivisions. One might almost characterize it as recitative style. As in a recitative the accompaniment serves as a commentary on the solo part, rather than mere rhythmic support.

The two instances where the piano has solo interludes, mm. 15 and 36, the writing calls for cadenza-like flourishes, rather than more melodic material. It is also noteworthy that at the opening of the movement, the flourishes are ascending and at the second statement they are descending, reflecting the mood and character of the solo part.

Proportion

It is exactly at m. 24, halfway through the piece, that the texture becomes denser between the parts and the piano has a clear-cut melody in octaves for the first time. As mentioned above, the opening has an irregular phrase structure, and from m. 21 onwards, it is clearly four-bar phrases, which shows Ben-Haim expressing a more placid character. All climaxes are well planned and the one at m. 36 which ends an entire section, is then articulated by the cascading, descending sextuplet 16ths.

Integrity

In large part, this piece is unified through the "spinning out" of the original irregular five-bar phrasing which calls for a spontaneous interpretation. Also the rhythmic indications mentioned above denoting the important sections are another factor of coherence. These rhythmical indications help create transitions which might otherwise contain rough seams.

At m. 25 with the melody in the piano part rather than in the solo part, and the new rhythmical material in the upper voice, is another binding motivic device. The cascade of sextuplet 16ths at mm. 37-40, mentioned above, is also a means of separating the end of a major section. All these elements work together to produce a work of contemplative longing.

Complexity

This piece has two themes, but there is much more contrast and complexity in the rhythmical scheme. The most tension occurs where the writing is the densest, mainly the middle of the movement, starting at mm. 24 through 36. There is much more rhythmic activity here than at the beginning as opposed to the simplicity of the opening and closing sections, which, as mentioned above, is transparent and sparse, and requires a more spontaneous interpretation.

This piece has much more give-and-take in it than the two works which precede it. The writing style is freer; many musical riches are derived from one theme.

Subtlety

The inclusion of an opening melody with three fermatas is certainly an interesting detail. Also the florid, cadenza-like passages interspersed throughout are an arresting feature of the work. Dropping down to *ppp* towards the end is a "trademark" of writing and the ending in E minor at the third measure from the end (m. 46) and then surprising the listener in the penultimate measure which is in the dominant, is an unusual turn of events. The cascading 16ths at m. 37, used to articulate between sections, is the result of highly skilled and subtle craftsmanship.

This particular work was originally conceived as a vocalise by Ben-Haim, but upon subsequent hearings, he decided to allow various instruments or voices to undertake the solo part.

Notes

1. Paul Ben-Haim, preface to the piano score of "Three Songs Without Words." (Tel-Aviv: Israeli Music Publications, 1952).
2. Paul Ben-Haim, preface to the 1953 edition of "Three Songs Without Words." (Tel Aviv: Israeli Music Publications, 1953).

Chapter Five

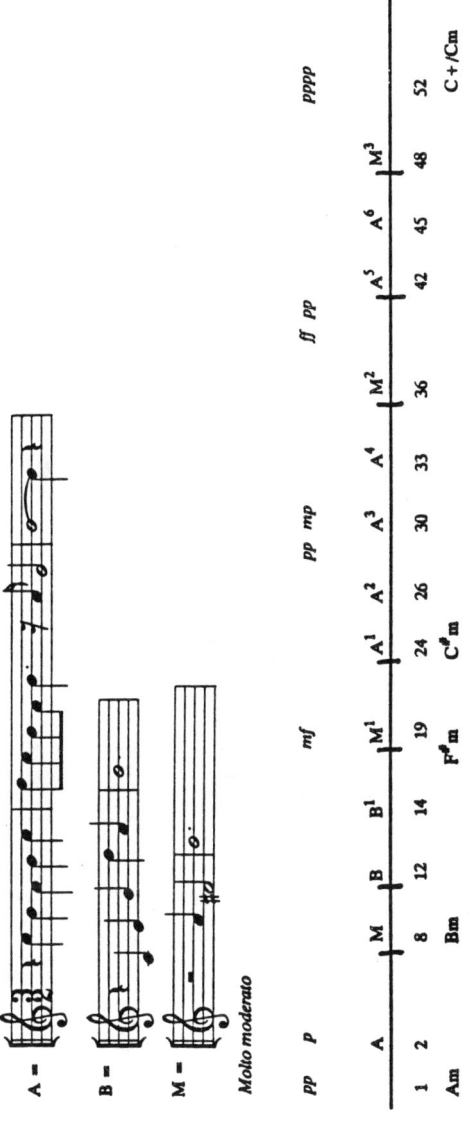

Three Songs Without Words. Ballad

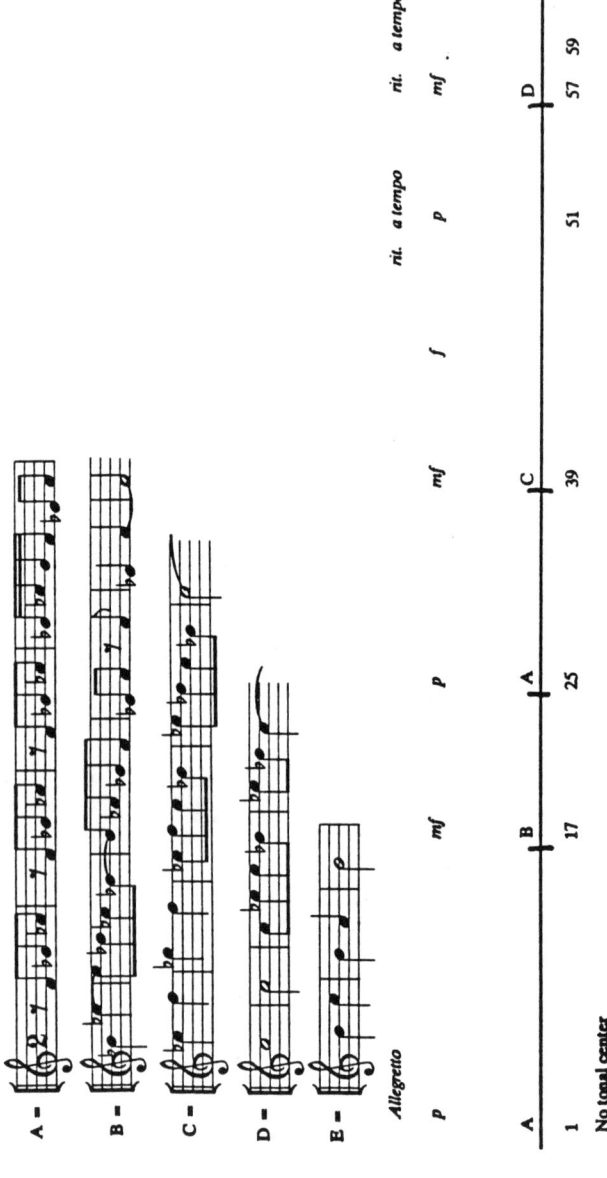

Chapter Five

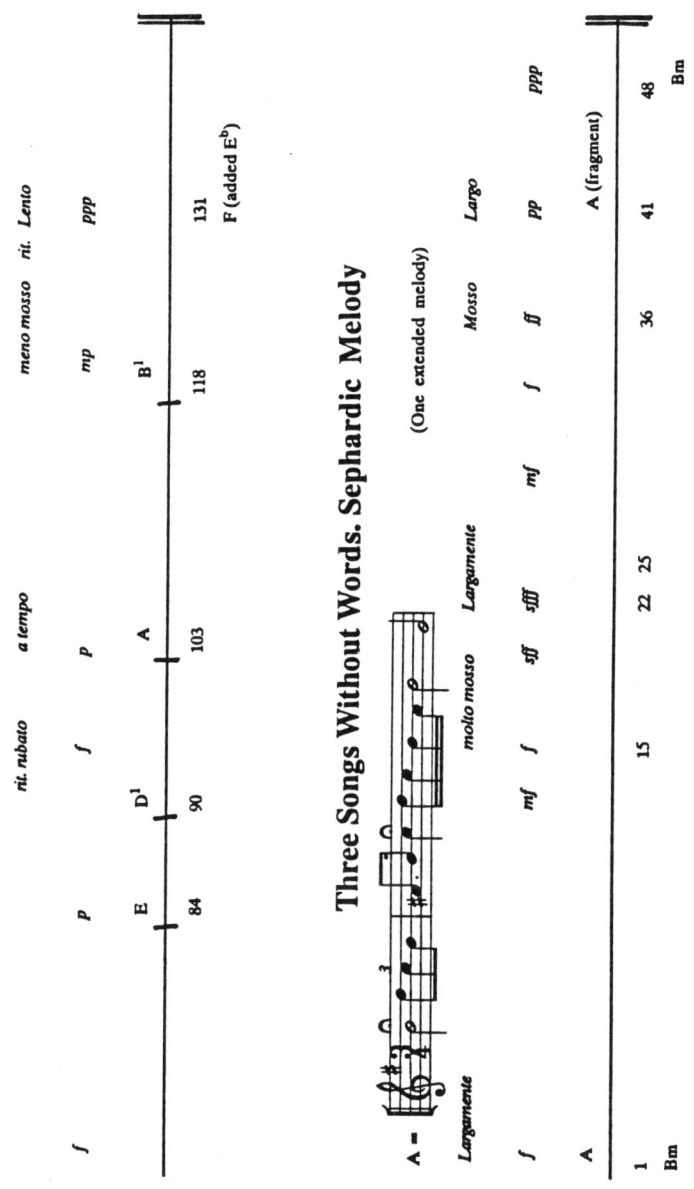

Chapter Six

VARIATIONS ON A HEBREW MELODY

Trio for Violin, Violoncello, and Pianoforte

1939

The *Variations on a Hebrew Melody* belong to Paul Ben-Haim's early Palestinian compositions. They were written in 1939 and are based on a tune known to the early settlers; it is probably of Bedouin origin.

The Theme and each variation of this work will be analyzed separately, as, unlike the Melody and Variations, this is a larger and more complex composition.

Introduction

Stylistic level

Sonority

This movement, which precedes the Theme, is an introduction, although Ben-Haim doesn't label it as such. Marked *adagio misterioso*, it is centered around the lower registers of the instruments, producing a mysterious and brooding quality. The piano's long trill, beginning with a *forte-pianissimo* gesture and concentrating mainly on the low G enhances this striking opening. The general effect dynamically is one of quiet intensity occasionally punctuated by outbursts of *forte* and, at the climax, (m. 32) a *fortissimo* from all three instruments.

The textures are sometimes transparent, as at the beginning, and sometimes denser, as at mm. 28-32. There are also instances of imitative counterpoint at mm. 2-15.

Harmony

Although the piano begins with a pedal point on G, it fails to establish any tonality because of the cello's entrance on G-sharp two beats later. There is no tonal center to this Introduction until m. 33 where C major seems to be established, but even here this key is contradicted by the violin's entrance on A-flat. It is only at the end that the key of G major is clearly established.

Rhythm

Although the time signature indicates common time, the only practical way to feel the rhythm of the opening cello part is to count eight eighth notes. This unique rhythm pattern is a binding motivic device and appears again and again as the various instruments take it up. The passage also consists of a written-out *accelerando*; the note values going from quarters to eighths to eighth-note triplets. This effect is enhanced by Ben-Haim's indication, *accelerando*, and contributes to the improvisatory character of the movement.

As the music grows in intensity, the beat increasingly subdivides, becoming 32nd note quintuplets (mm. 28, 30) which is the build-up to the climax of the entire piece at m. 32, as mentioned above.

Melody

The melody begins disjunctly, then becomes conjunct, moving in chromatic steps, and finally ending as it began with disjunct movement. These half-steps give the melody a distinctly oriental flavor. There are also fugal sections at mm 5 and 11.

The descending major sixth, ascending minor seventh skips which are a regular feature of the opening motif are abandoned at the cello's entrance at m. 24. It should be noted that although the melody has a disjunct-conjunct-disjunct pattern, it is still within a regular four-bar phrasing.

At mm. 43-44, Ben-Haim anticipates the Theme's first three notes by simply using those same three notes (B, A, G) as an ending to the Introduction, first in quarter notes and then rhythmically augmented with half notes. Superimposed on this is a retrograde version (E-flat, F, G) played by the piano.

Structural level

Clarity

The formal design of this Introduction is very freely realized and does not fit into a pre-determined pattern. The piece shows a certain sense of order, in that important sections are delineated by means of solo piano episodes, mm.12 and 33.

There is a distinct contrast in the work's texture. The first large section up to m. 32, builds to a rather dense sound and is thinned out at the return of the opening at m. 34.

Proportion

The entire piece is dominated by the rhythmic figure:

Example 9. *Variations on a Hebrew Melody*, m. 1.

except for the eight-measure section beginning one measure after rehearsal letter A. At m. 23, which is exactly half way through the movement, the rhythmic figure reappears, with the melody somewhat varied. After the climax at m. 32, the return of the original idea is accompanied by a more rhapsodic piano accompaniment.

Integrity

The music is cohesive, despite the frequency of clearly delineated areas. Ben-Haim's use of two main motifs, (mm. 1, 16) gives a strong sense of unity and coherence within the movement.
 Transitions are easy to hear because of the composer's use of the piano alone, which introduces the new sections each time they appear (m.12, 33). It may be concluded that this device promotes extremely smooth movement from one section to another.

Complexity

As there are only two main musical ideas, there is not a great amount of melodic contrast in this movement. However, dynamics, and textural differences provide some variety. The second idea, played by the piano, clearly anticipates the melody of the Theme.

Subtlety

Although this piece is not in an identifiable key, the composer departs from this norm by ending in G major, clearly preparing the way for the Theme. There are few surprises dynamically, except for the very first trilled note in the piano, which is marked *fpp*.
 Other than these examples, Ben-Haim colors his music in a gentle and subdued fashion.

Theme

Stylistic Level

Sonority

The main body of the piece begins with a quiet, gentle statement of the Theme, marked *tranquillo*, played in unison by the violin and cello. Even though the piano enters with octaves, (m. 59) the soft dynamics are maintained. The piano does provide a denser texture at m. 72, giving the music more depth, while still keeping it within a low dynamic range.

Harmony

The theme is clearly in the key of C-sharp minor. For most of the section, there is unison texture which implies various harmonies without specifically establishing any of them. Two pivotal points where the piano speaks out strongly are the dominant, G-sharp, at mm. 59 and 72. There are also several instances of the use of pedal point.

Rhythm

While the Introduction was in 4/4 time, the Theme is in triple meter. Its simple, regular, unpretentious rhythm patterns are in keeping with the largely unison presentation of the Theme. The tempo should in no way be rushed, a caution reinforced by the *moderato* marking at the beginning. Excessive dragging can be avoided by following the composer's direction, *breve* above each fermata.

Melody

The most obvious melodic feature of the Theme is the three notes in the first measure which are followed by a nearly exact inverted version in the third measure (m. 49). The augmented fifth glissando, suggestive of quarter tones, gives the melody a Middle-Eastern quality. Melodic elaboration and chromaticism are also evident at mm. 45-50. There is also a clear instance of imitative counterpoint beginning at m. 62, furnishing a striking contrast to the stark austerity of the previous unison statement.

Structural Level

Clarity

The Theme consists of two basic ideas, presented as short melodic fragments together forming one phrase of four bars each. This is repeated twice and ends at m. 54. There are eight bars of antecedent and eight bars of consequent phrasing. M. 58 ends on a high C-sharp and m. 62 ends on the same note an octave lower.

Proportion

The Theme is 32 measures long. Exactly at mid-point, m. 59, we have the beginning of the contrapuntal episode mentioned above.

The first statement of the Theme is made up of 12 measures, which ends with a dotted half-note and a fermata. This segment is divided into three four-bar phrases. The middle section (59-71) is uneven in its phrase structure. At m. 72 up to the end, there is an even 8-bar period consisting of two 4-bar phrases.

Integrity

The first twelve measures which contain two phrases, comprise all the melodic material of the Theme. These two phrases (A and B) unify the piece motivically, and reoccur continually throughout the statement of the Theme.

As in classical variation forms, both elements of the Theme are repeated.

Complexity

Ben-Haim is extremely frugal in his use of melodic material. Not only are the themes short and simple, but they are repeated. The first part is rhythmically more varied with its use of glissando and eighth notes, while the second part is simply unadorned quarter notes.

Subtlety

In most examples of the form of Theme and Variation, the theme itself is usually stark and simple, giving the composer room for manipulation. This is also true of Ben-Haim's Theme, making it quite straightforward and predictable. The one departure from this norm is the episode of imitative counterpoint.

Variation I

Stylistic Level

Sonority

The overall impression of the first variation's sonority is subdued, as in many of Ben-Haim's works. The range of dynamics includes
ppp to *forte*. Except for a few instances of *sforzando*, the true climax starts at m. 99 and builds to *forte* and m. 106. There is one more outburst of *forte* at m. 114, but this is quickly reversed with the last measure marked *"ppp."*
The first sixteen measures use the upper half of the piano keyboard, the next thirteen use more of the bass range, and finally the piece ends in the high register again.

Harmony

Although the harmony is nontraditional, this variation clearly begins and ends in the key of G-sharp minor. The variation is an example of Ben-Haim's style of writing Oriental-derived modal melodies with Western-sounding harmonies.

Rhythm

There are several changes of meter in this variation, shifting from duple to triple and back again. The three quarter notes which dominate the Theme are again in evidence here, unchanged and unvaried, although the accompaniment patterns are much more elaborate. Between the quarter-note motifs there is much rhythmic subdivision, mainly sixteenths and thirty-second notes. Unlike the Theme which maintains a strict tempo, this variation has a very flexible beat, with *ritards, rubatos* and *accelerandos.*

Melody

The three quarter notes which dominate the Theme dominate this first variation as well. The upward and downward step-wise movement is also reiterated here. The rhythmic subdivisions in eighth-notes found in the Theme are developed further by using sixteenth and thirty-second note runs.

Structural Level

Clarity

This first variation is based on both ideas presented in the Theme. However, the writing is improvisatory in style and more florid in pianistic techniques. Formally, it is divided into two main sections, the second of which starts at m. 106. There is a short coda (m. 117), which paves the way for Variation II.

Proportion

In spite of the fact that the writing is more florid and rhapsodic, the eight-measure phrase structure is maintained throughout most of this variation. The major deviation from this is a kind of codetta which Ben-Haim appends to end of the Variation, marked *ritenuto*, which leads to an *adagio* ending. The climax of the variation, m. 106, is the one place in Variation I where theme B is alluded to.

Integrity

This variation is unified through the use of the ascending and descending quarter-note motif found in the very first measure. The other motif, at m. 99, is an inversion of the opening one and is displaced by one beat.

Complexity

Although the two motifs are structurally simple, they are treated differently in terms of texture. The opening one is made up of single quarters with a counter melody in the left hand part. Both are in the higher register of the piano. The other motif is not only in the lower register, but is made up of chords, with an ostinato accompaniment in the bass. This change of register also creates a distinct change of mood; the beginning is tuneful and transparent, the other motif is dark and mysterious.

Subtlety

Although this variation has a number of meter changes, the phrases flow into each other naturally. The one place that deviates from this pattern is at m. 114 where the right hand breaks into a cadenza-like run and together with the left hand, ends the piece with a unison melody.

Variation II

Stylistic Level

Sonority

In the variation the piano is reunited with the violin and cello. The sonorities are light and transparent, like a scherzo — a strong contrast to the previous material. The first climax at m. 137 is reinforced the other climax at m. 150 the piano's runs cascade by an upward thirty second-note run in the piano, while the other climax at m. 150 the piano's runs cascade downward.

Harmony

In the beginning, the key of A minor is implied; however, the left hand with its seconds and thirds clashes with this harmony. Because of this, one is hard-pressed to identify a specific tonal center. As is often the case, harmonies are often more implied than explicitly stated. The prevailing texture in this variation is polyphonic, although the piano part is less so.

Rhythm

The tempo indication *allegretto grazzioso* sets the spritely, light-hearted mood of this work. The violin introduces the first motif, this time with an upbeat, which is the Theme in diminution, embellished with trills. As the music builds toward a climax from mm. 145 to 150, the piano part has increasingly subdivided beats, eventually erupting with thirty second-note sextuplets at the moment of greatest expressiveness.

Melody

The opening motif (the Theme in diminution) is repeated three times, and this happens every time it appears (with slight variation) in both the piano and string parts. At m. 130, the original version of the Theme appears in the violin part, and at m. 134, both the original and diminished versions are juxtaposed. The piano part at m. 145 begins a variant of the diminished version of the Theme, heard earlier and culminates in the climax of the variation at m. 150.

Unlike the first variation, this work's range which centers around the middle registers of the instruments remains the same throughout.

Structural Level

Clarity

This variation uses the idea of rhythmic diminution and applies to the A part of the Theme. What was

Example 10. *Theme*, mm. 49-50.

becomes

Example 11. *Variation II*, mm. 120-121.

Throughout the movement, Ben-Haim also combines the two elements (A and B) of the Theme at mm. 138 and 144.

The melody which started out plain and melancholy has now been transformed into a dance-like statement of grace and light heartedness, possessing a scherzando quality.

Proportion

Because of the clarity of the writing, the ingenious combining of two versions of the Theme — original and diminished, is easy to hear.

The structure of this variation consists of three-bar phrase groups, except for two instances; one is the end of a climactic *forte* section, where the phrases fall into groups of four (mm. 150-153). The other is the concluding four measures, which lends a logical and cohesive balance to this variation.

Integrity

As mentioned above, the main integrating element in this variation is the diminished version of the Theme juxtaposed with the original version. This thematic material constantly permeates the fabric of the music and provides rhythmic, harmonic and melodic synchronization throughout the variation. An interesting detail is the recalling of the piano's opening accompanying pattern at mm. 155-158.

Complexity

There is a distinct contrast between the complexity of the piano writing and the comparatively simple string parts. The piano has much greater rhythmic variety as well as sharper technical demands.

The diminished version of the Theme is staccato and playful in character, but the original version played by the violin, requires a broad, expansive, legato quality.

Subtlety

The concinnity of all the elements projects an aura of the fantastic and is sustained by the intricate melodic weaving of the various versions of the Theme. Also noteworthy is the extending of the second part of the theme by a cadenza in the violin (m. 151). The music ends, so characteristic of Ben-Haim by fading away to a whisper, accentuated by the otherworldly quality of the harmonics in the violin and cello.

Variation III

Stylistic Level

Sonority

Although this piece begins *pianissimo*, with Stravinsky-like unison chords, a quiet energy is sensed due to the staccato markings and the rests between the chords. The piano continues this military march, occasionally enhanced by embellishments which punctuate the sound.

The cello enters with a statement marked *forte* and *non legato* which denotes a marked change from the previous variations. There are many instances of *forte* and louder passages throughout, highlighting the vehement nature of this variation.

Harmony

The harmony of the opening section seems to be establishing the key of D minor and the ending is clearly A major. Except for these places, however, harmonic stability is not an important element in this variation. The texture is far thicker than any previous variation and in a measure such as 193-4 there is much going on harmonically, rhythmically, and melodically. Namely, the two sixteenths and an eighth rhythm in the string parts, a quarter note melody above sextuplet sixteenths in the right-hand-piano part and eighths in the left-hand piano part.

Rhythm

The tempo indication *alla marcia* creates a mood of force and determination, which is exemplified by the Stravinsky-like syncopated chords in the opening measures. The meter changes frequently throughout this variation, avoiding a predictable beat grouping and making the music more compelling. The rhythmic motif in m. 122 of Variation II is further exploited at m. 202 in Variation III.

Melody

The opening cello statement, with its tied half-note followed by 16th note runs, is a motif which is carried out quite consistently throughout the variation in all three parts. Nearly every phrase begins with a long note followed by shorter ones.

There are two main themes which comprise this variation, and they are in direct contrast to each other. Namely, the first theme at m. 172 in the cello is rambling and improvisatory in nature, while the second theme at m. 184 is strident and martial in character.

Structural Level

Clarity

This variation is in stark contrast to the mood of previous one. The march-like chords, articulated by rests, with which it opens are marked *molto staccato* and *pianissimo*, producing a mysterious and menacing atmosphere. The cello part beginning at m. 172 is not related to the Theme, but at m. 184, the string parts are clearly derived from the B part of the Theme.

Proportion

This variation consists of 48 measures and it is noteworthy that exactly half way through the movement, starting at m. 192 Ben-Haim creates a climax by bringing together all the motivic devices which comprise this work. The right-hand piano part sings out the variant of the opening theme above sextuplets 16th notes, while the string parts punch away at the motif derived from Variation II mentioned above.

Integrity

The figure:

Example 12. *Theme*, m. 59

is a binding motivic device and is derived from the second part of the Theme, m. 59. This idea also appears in the piano part in a different guise in mm.193-4, and in the violin at m. 199. The cello's opening statement consisting of a long note followed by shorter ones is also a consistent element unifying the variation motivically.

The coordination of musical elements within this variation, as opposed to what came before, is very different in its conception and effect. From the Theme on, the opening measures all included three quarter notes or three related eighth notes, but in this variation, the opening is distinctly different with its open intervals and unison chromatic progressions.

Complexity

In the large context, the two main motifs represent a strong contrast to one another. The first one, the cello's entrance at m. 172, is primarily free and improvisatory. The second motif at m. 182, played by the strings in unison, is forceful and strident in effect.

In observing the relationship between complexities and simplicities and to tensions and releases, it is noteworthy that this variation is for the most part complex in all its musical materials. Such an example is m. 210 which brings together and expands upon the opening cello part, m. 172. The few transparent textures (m. 199) are obfuscated by the busy piano part.

Subtlety

The listener is intrigued by the opening measures of this variation which feature a highly syncopated rhythm pattern unlike anything that came before. This pattern, exclusively in the piano, continues up to m. 184. An interesting ornamental touch is the glissando in the last measure of the piano part.

Variation IV

Stylistic Level

Sonority

Compared to the previous variation, this one maintains a somewhat lower dynamic level. Although it starts strongly, its penultimate measure is marked with three *p's*. The climax of the variation, marked *forte* occurs at m. 230, where the three eighth notes and the triplet sixteenths in the piano part interact to produce a primitive sound akin to a drum beat. This figure appears earlier (m. 221) also in the piano part; however, it is part of a larger context and is marked *piano*.

Harmony

The variation tends toward the key of A minor; however, there are many places where there is no tonal center. The prevailing texture is polyphonic, which is not the case with the previous variations; they tend toward homophony. At the climax, m. 230, the "drum" theme is heard for the first time as a completely chromatic structure.

Rhythm

The 8/4 time signature is unusual, but as mentioned in the Performance Guide it shows Ben-Haim's desire for a continuous dialogue and a long, uninterrupted melodic line between the instruments. Unlike previous variations, there is no change of meter and few tempo changes.

Melody

There is a parallel between the Theme's three descending quarters and the pizzicato eighths in the cello part. Other relationships to the Theme are found in the violin part at m. 219, the last three beats, and at m. 221, the violin part, starting on beat four. The most striking feature of the melody is the triplet 16th figure which is derived from Variation III, and is balanced by the longer note values which follow.

A melody which appears toward the end of this variation in the violin (m. 233) is in direct contrast to the mysterious, drum-like figure in the piano. It is dreamy and legato and climbs to the register of the instrument.

Structural Level

Clarity

This variation fragments the Theme more than any of the previous ones. Only here and there can snatches melody be related to anything familiar. There are two main ideas dominating this section and they are presented simultaneously:

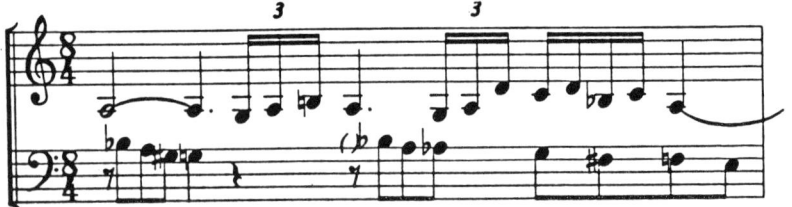

Example 13. *Variation IV*, m. 217.

Proportion

Exactly half way through the variation the opening idea is recalled one step higher in an expanded variant, this time featuring a different piano accompaniment. At m. 230, three quarters of the way through the movement, comes the climax, which, in the violin part, is a further expansion of the opening material. A common thread running through this whole set of variations is that something significant happens half way through.

Integrity

This variation is more highly integrated than the rest, concentrating on two main ideas, the triplet sixteenths and the three eighths notes.

The concinnity of the elements are employed carefully through an interweaving of melodic, sonorous, and rhythmic components.

Complexity

The amount and degree of contrast employed in this work, may be considered less striking than in the previous variations. The continuation of the melody is closely connected to the opening idea because no new material is introduced which may be considered truly original.

In this variation Ben-Haim balances a simple melodic line in the violin with a more rhythmically intricate part in the piano. This creates a tension between the instruments which is resolved at the end by a gradual fragmenting of the motifs and a fading away to almost nothing, or as Ben-Haim directs, *quasi niente*.

Subtlety

This is the first instance where there is no break between sections or a fermata at the end of a section; the music leads directly into Variation V. Also, as mentioned above, the 8/4 meter is an unusual device which helps to promote longer phrase structures and a more compelling internal propulsion.

Variation V

Stylistic Level

Sonority

This work is unlike any other in the set; the composer indicates not only *Molto vivace*, but also *tempestoso* in his opening tempo marking. Although he begins *pianissimo,* ten measures into the piece there is a *subito forte* which lasts until m. 245. The impression of this variation's sonority is anything but subdued, despite the fact that the piece begins and ends softly.

Harmony

The opening of Variation V with its meandering 8th notes interweaving between the scale-wise passages in the various instruments, clearly has no tonal center.

At the beginning and at the end, however, there are places that do point to certain harmonies. In the string parts the melody in octaves starting at m. 248 until 260 is clearly in A flat major; however, the piano part contradicts this, and at rehearsal L (m. 260), it starts in B-flat with both hands and clearly ends in E-flat in m. 263, although whether major or minor is impossible to determine. There is a toccata-like passage starting at m. 277 which is clearly in B-flat major but by the time it gets to m. 279, a few measures later, there is again no tonal center. The next key center, A major, begins at m. 294 and does seem to circle around A major until m. 313 which is in E-minor. The last measure, although it is in no particular key, has a very strong pull toward either B-major or B-minor and, in fact, the following variation begins in E- major, for which the previous tonality of B could be dominant preparation.

It can be seen that in this variation, there is no key which is strongly established. However, there is an intensification of various keys throughout the work which are obscured very shortly after they are introduced.

There is much imitation in the beginning; for example m. 240 in the cello part which is then taken up by the piano. The rest of the variation is more homophonic in texture.

Rhythm

This variation is mainly in triple meter. There are several rhythmic changes towards the end, starting at m. 278, but triple meter predominates. The rhythmic design of this variation is Broque in concept because of the contrast between long and short notes being played against each other.

In transitional sections, such as m. 277, a toccata-like pattern is employed and at climaxes, such as mm. 294-303, chordal writing is used, although the variation does not begin this way. The chordal writing which does occur has the same purpose as the initial contrapuntal idea — running notes against longer ones. An example of this can be found at mm. 299-303.

Melody

Although there are some sections where fragments of the melody occur, for the most part when melody appears in any of the instrumental parts it is usually a long statement. For instance, the melody is introduced in the violin part starting at m. 248, and going until m. 267. It is also introduced in octaves and at m. 260 it is open fifths while the piano part has an almost jazzy "walking bass." At m. 270 the theme is in the piano part which is a variation and elaboration of the original Theme. This goes on from m. 272 to 277. Then we get a suggestion of the Theme in augmentation at m. 294 and at m. 306 the Theme is doubly augmented.

From m. 316 to 324, we have a very elongated version of the Theme, again in the string parts, but it is made up of fragments only. As the music intensifies the registration gets much higher, for example m. 308. Also the density of the texture increases from mm. 294 to 303, another climax. It is noteworthy that at m. 248 the melody in the violins is an augmentation of the Theme, while the melody at m. 316 is a diminution of the same Theme.

Structural Level

Clarity

The Theme is played by the violin in pizzicato octaves in an augmented version, contrasting with Variation II which presents the Theme in diminution.

A variant on the original version is heard on the piano at m. 270.

Except for a short toccata-like interlude starting at m. 274 and continuing in a slightly changed version at m. 287, the main theme returns with a much denser texture. The final variation is ushered in after a measure of prolonged silence.

Proportion

Just by counting the measures, one can see that this is the longest variation, consisting of 97 measures. Exactly half way through at m. 287, with a return to 3/4 time, there is a return to the beginning for the preparation of the main climax at m. 303, and this starts exactly in the middle of the variation. About three quarters of the way through the variation, at m. 313, is an *a tempo* marking which just followed a *largamente* marking and is another significant climax.

The concinnity of the elements is the result of an intricate design integrating melody, rhythm, and harmony. Everything comes together in this movement to produce a vital and lucid amalgam.

Integrity

Through the use of long, flowing melodic statements and scale-wise "walking basses," this piece achieves unity and coherence, making it an entity which is different from all that came before. Because of its length and design the concinnity of formal elements is consistently adhered to. For example, the opening with its interweaving accompaniment from one instrument to the other quickly develops into a more weighty statement (m. 244). The combination of components, such as contrapuntal and homophonic movement, often come together in a unifying statement. Mm. 248-267 will exemplify this idea. Important sections are clearly delineated through the use of interweaving musical materials.

Complexity

This movement is fiery and extroverted in mood. Strong contrast is represented through the use of the insistent octave melody in the violin starting at m. 243 punctuated by rests, while the piano has a busy, staccato collaboration. There is consistent use of long notes or long chords against faster moving counter melodies. This idea starts out simply and then is expanded into chordal texture. There are several in stances of melodic fragmentation starting at m. 316.

Basically there are two ideas in this variation, one consisting of long notes, the other of shorter notes.

Subtlety

There is not much use of subtle writing in this variation, however, the section marked *martellato* at m. 276 is different. This transitional section is toccata-like, the intervals are very close together and the idea is unlike what has gone before.

An interesting detail is the use of the tritone, which is found throughout this work and is prominent just before the *Grosse Pause* of m. 335. This recalls the tritone heard in the second measure of the Theme.

Variation VI

Stylistic Level

Sonority

With this variation, the composer returns to a dynamic level of subdued intensity. The opening is *pianissimo* and the closing dynamic for the entire piece is *pppp*. Also significant is the indication of *Molto tranquillo* an atmosphere of calm of peacefulness, creating a sharp contrast to the tempestuous Fifth Variation. The only point where there is a *forte* is in the cello part, m. 354 and it is not a significant moment, simply the climax of the cello line, not a climax for all three parts. In fact, the climactic points in this piece are at its softest moments. A significant section where the Theme comes back at Tempo I, (m. 361) is only marked *mezzo piano*. Because of these effects, the whole movement has a dream-like quality.

Harmony

This piece is more tonal in concept than the other variations have been. It begins in what could be either E minor or E major — the mode is ambiguous — with an insistently reiterated motif:

Example 14. *Variation VI*, m. 336.

At m. 356 the theme of the Introduction is recalled for the first time since its initial appearance, and at m. 361, the Theme in its original setting is recapitulated in all the parts in unison. It is in the original key of C-sharp minor and clearly ends in that key.

Rhythm

There are four main sections of this work which have a significant tempo or expression marking. The first is the opening,

Molto tranquillo, which harks back to Ben-Haim's pastoral style. Next, there is the reiteration of the Introduction's opening theme at m. 356, marked *movendo* (moving), then the return of the original Theme in its original key at Tempo I, and finally the last page marked *piu lento.* where the Theme is heard one last time double augmented and fading away to nothing.

The meter is 3/4 for most of the beginning, with a few deviations into 5/4. It changes to 4/4 when the theme of the Introduction is recalled, and then back to 3/4 at Tempo I for the recapitulation of the Theme upon which the variations are based.

Melody

Melodically the opening of this variation resembles an impressionistic nocturne with its arpeggiated bass. A significant feature of the melody is the first two notes which are an open fifth. This interval is exploited throughout the variation, melodically as well as harmonically. The opening phrase is heard in almost every measure until m. 351 and then is brought back at the very end in mm. 381-382.

There are three main themes in the variation. The first is the cello's, beginning at m. 344, a theme which bears a strong resemblance to a cantor's chant. The second appears at m. 356, the theme of the Introduction, and the third is return of the original Theme at m. 361 which is further elaborated upon in the *piu lento* section at the end.

Structural Level

Clarity

There are three main divisions to this work. The first section uses a motif which is introduced in the first measure and is repeated almost constantly until m. 351. Then an interlude containing a cantorial-like chant starts at m. 352 and flows into a reprise of the theme of the Introduction at m. 356. The second division occurs at m. 361 where there is a restatement of the complete theme in its original key and meter. Finally a third section, marked *Piu lento* brings the whole work to a quiet close.

Proportion

This last variation is symmetrical in its design. There are three sections, the most important of which occurs almost exactly in the middle at m. 361. Also, three quarters of the way through (m. 373) there begins an embellishment of the original theme.

Because this is a summation of all that has gone before, the mood is quietly contemplative and there is no real climax as such.

Integrity

Throughout the variation there are quotations of the work's prominent themes; at m. 356 is the opening idea from the Introduction and at m. 361 a statement of the Theme itself. This confluence of ideas is an element which gives coherence to the entire work.

The motif quoted in Example 14, p. 159, is also a unifying idea which binds the whole variation together, appearing prominently in all the sections and for the last time, only four measures before the end.

Complexity

There are no sharp contrasts in this last variation. There is a mood of quiet introspection as the music reviews some of the themes which have been manipulated during the course of the work. Two themes seem to be new and unrelated to anything that came before. One was quoted above, the other appears in the cello part at m. 344 and is elaborated upon in the piano part starting at m. 366.

Subtlety

The original theme is quoted at m. 361 but without the falling augmented 4th, making it seem more positive. On the last page beginning at m. 373, there is a final elaboration of the Theme and at m. 378 a statement in augmentation of its first three notes marked *morendo sin al Fine*, a typical Ben-Haim ending, fading off into nothingness.

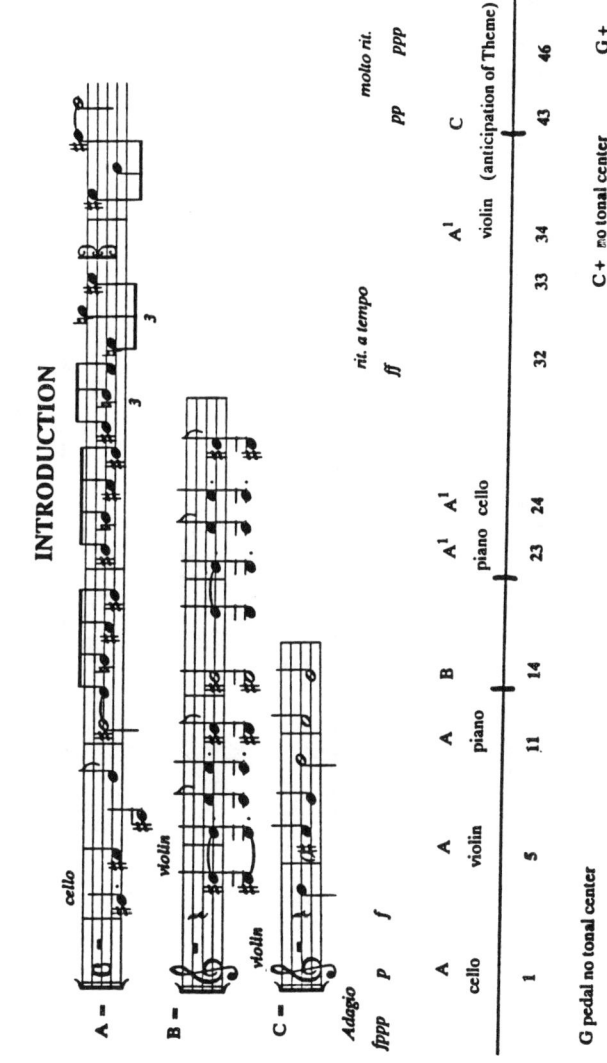

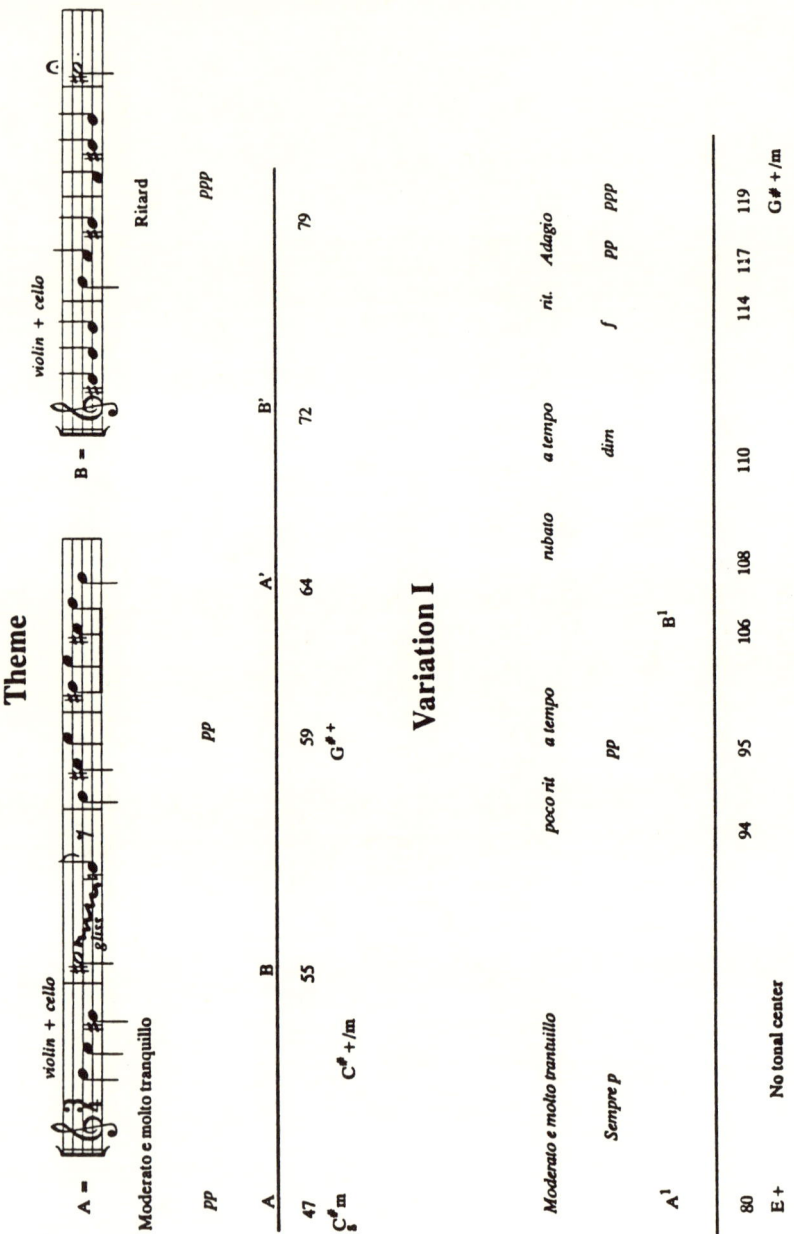

125

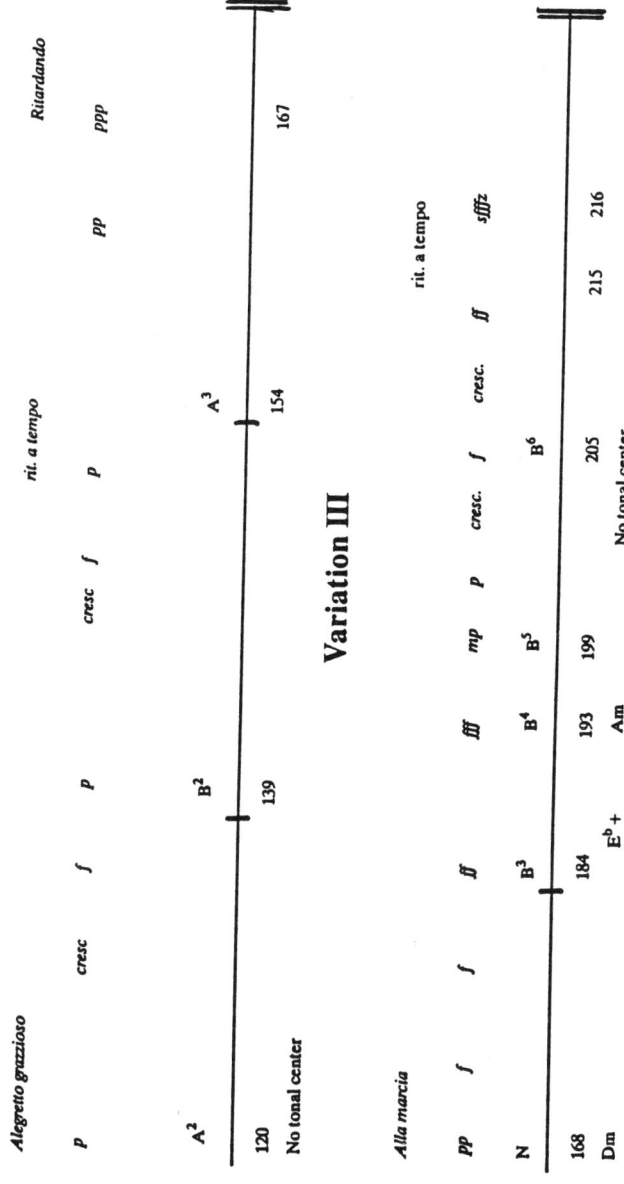

Variation IV

Moderato   rall. a tempo   rit. a tempo

f   p   ff   f   pp   ppp

A⁴

217   223   225   237
Am   Em   No tonal center

Variation V

Molto vivace   Laragmente a tempo   rit. a tempo

pp   f   p   cresc   f   ff   mp ff   fff   sfz p

A⁵   B⁷

238   260   274   287   301   313   323   335
No tonal center   B♭+   N.T.C.   Em   N.T.C.

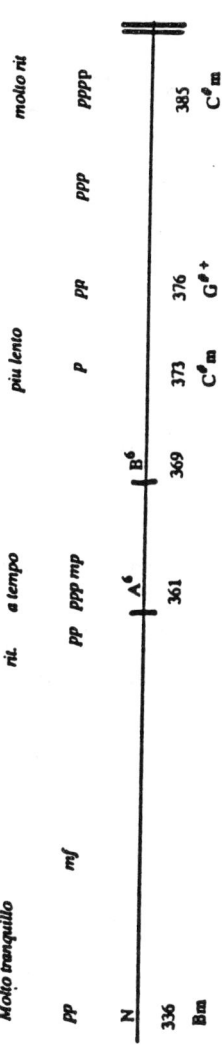

Chapter Seven

QUINTET

FOR CLARINET AND STRING QUARTET

1937

After having written large-scale works such as the *First Symphony* (1940) and having it successfully received, the composer felt the need to create a quieter, more lyrical work. He finished the *Quintet* in 1941. This work is a continuation of early and new ways of writing.

The earlier style of writing (as in the *First Symphony*) which immediately preceded the Quintet continued the Romantic tradition, while the chamber music featured two kinds of writing, namely, pastoral and dance-like, with touches of folk music.[1]

First Movement

Stylistic Level

Sonority

The sonority of this movement runs to extremes; from *pppp* (m. 27) to *fortissimo* (mm. 134 and 250) but in general the dynamic level is quiet. At m. 134, which is near the beginning of the Development section, there is the first *fortissimo* which provides the most powerful climax of the movement up to that point. The next significant climax occurs in the Recapitulation section at m.

250 which is a restatement of the second Theme in truncated form.

When introducing the three main sections of the sonata form — exposition, development and recapitulation, Ben-Haim uses a more transparent texture than in the rest of the work, adding mystery and significance to these important structural landmarks. It is interesting to note that the composer ends the movement in the same manner as he began it, with a repeated C in the viola, accompanied only by the cello.

Harmony

The movement clearly begins and ends in C major. Sections containing bi-tonality, such as m. 52 may be found.

Written in a contemporary style, this piece is not clear-cut traditional harmonic practice. Primitive sounding open fifths are found from m. 289 to the end, as well as at m. 125 in the bass. The Recapitulation which normally returns to the home tonic has an abundance of C's in supporting parts, while the clarinet sings its part in the key of E-flat.

Rhythm

There are frequent changes of meter in the first movement, but tempo changes occur less often. The one-bar shifts of meter are used primarily to elongate phrases. Starting at m. 135 in the section which relates to mm. 77-78, there are frequent meter changes and quite unusual ones, such as 7/8 and 5/8, This goes on from m. 135 to 146, with almost constant shifts of meter. Then it is back to the 3/4 time with which the work opens, with an occasional variant here and there until the end. Ben-Haim is also quite frugal with his tempo changes. The opening is marked *molto moderato* with several *poco ralantandos* and *a tempos* spanning a measure or two (for example mm. 49-51, mm. 75-77), and then there is a long *ralantando molto* just before the development at m. 112.

One very significant tempo marking, which gives a good clue to the character of this work and to its interpretation are the words *leggierissimo e scherzando* at m. 210, with the repeated spiccato note accompaniment in the violas. A quiet drama is created in the opening and throughout the piece with the use of repeated short notes, like those in the viola mentioned above juxtaposed with a long-lined and contemplative melody in the clarinet part. Rhythmically, an important feature of this work is the opening clarinet melody which starts with a dotted half-note tied to a dotted eighth followed by two thirty seconds and two quarters.

Example 15. *1st Movement*, mm. 1-2.

Such a distinctive rhythm pattern stands out whenever it appears. This idea is broadened at m. 20 with the use of a pedal point on the note F in the bass for seven measures against scherzando-like writing in the viola and violin parts.

Melody

This rather lengthy first movement is made up of only two themes, the opening theme and the second theme starting at m. 63. The opening theme is lyrical with a yearning quality; an outstanding feature is the long dotted half-notes tied to another dotted eighth followed by very quick thirty-second-notes. The theme starts out diatonically, then accidentals are used in various spots. The next time this theme is heard in the clarinet, is at m.

51, this time one step lower. The words *un poco pronunziato* indicates that the composer wishes the playing to be more emphatic than at the opening.

At m. 63, the Second Theme is introduced which is actually an elaboration and variation of the First Theme, this time employing sextuplet thirty-second- notes to embellish the melody. The main theme is then re-introduced at m. 112, this time in the first violin part in a key one step higher than the opening. It is noteworthy that the theme, when it is repeated in a higher key, is at a significant structural member, in this instance, the Development, m. 112.

At the Recapitulation, m. 199, the main theme is restated at a higher register, thus heightening the emotional impact of this restatement. One of the few places that contrasts with the prevailing light-hearted mood occurs at the beginning of the coda, m. 276, marked *misterioso*. Typically the ending dies away to a whisper.

Structural Level

Clarity

The structure of the movement follows the classical sonata form, except for the fact that there is no repeat of the Exposition. The Second Theme is clearly projected by the clarinet at m. 63 and the Development begins at m. 112. At the Recapitulation, m. 199, the pulsating pedal point is modified through the use of harmonics above the repeated notes as well as rests which interrupt the steady flow of eighth-notes.

There is a distinct contrast in how the composer conceived his opening gesture. It is accomplished through the use of a long-lined, almost static clarinet melody against pulsating C's in the viola part. It is further enhanced with a somewhat slower moving C pedal point an octave lower in the cello.

Proportion

Although nothing musically significant happens exactly in the middle of the piece, architecturally something quite interesting is occurring; from the Second Theme to the Development takes 49 measures, mm. 63 to 112. From the first climax to the second theme also takes 49 measures, mm. 133-182, making the structure very symmetrical thus far. From the recapitualtion to the Second Theme, which is also the second climax, is 51 measures — close to 49. From the Second Theme to the coda, mm. 250 to 275 is 25 measures and the coda mm. 275 to 301 (the end of the first movement) is 26 measures; added up, there are 51 measures again. So we find a remarkable symmetry in the structural underpinning to this music. The climaxes as well as the rest of the work are a result of a logical and cohesive design.

Integrity

This first movement is mainly integrated through its first and second themes, being both similar and contrasting in rhythmical and intervalic content. Melodically the first theme's notes are quite close, never moving more than the interval of a second apart. In the first phrase rhythmically, there is an inherent contrast with the use of a long dotted half note tied over to a dotted eighth, immediately followed by thirty second notes, and then by quarters. This in itself immediately produces tension, especially when played against the repeated, pulsating notes in the viola part. It is only phrase by phrase that the intervals in the melody of the clarinet begin to expand.

In the second theme, starting at m. 63, there is an immediate emotional upswing with the use of the interval of the octave (E) ascending, then followed by a melody which is more conjunct but still further apart than the opening, intervalically.

Rhythmically, the music is an expansion and elaboration of what came before, although it starts out with a similar rhythm. The theme is expanded with 16th-notes in m. 64 and at m. 66, there are the 32nd-note sextuplets, upon which the rhythm is now based. The four 16ths in m. 64, which is a device first introduced by the clarinet in m. 35, is expanded further in mm. 72- 73; then at m. 89 there is a long statement of these repeated groups of four 16ths. This idea is greatly expanded upon in most of the instrumental parts.

Ben-Haim further integrates his material at the development section. For instance, at m. 112 there is a reversal of the main theme, a reminder of the opening in the first violin section, while the clarinet has the repeated pulsating notes the viola originally had, with some interruption by rests. At m. 117, this idea is further expanded through the use of grace notes. In transitional material such as that at m. 136, the rhythm is related to the beginning, although a livelier rhythm pattern is used.

The techniques mentioned earlier are in fact used throughout the movement, either for the main theme or for transitional material; the conjunct melodies are followed shortly thereafter by melodies with notes of a larger distance, rhythms characterized by long notes followed by short 32nds, and grace notes and trills as at m. 265 in the cello. The coordination of these elements works together to produce an atmosphere of mystery balanced by sunnier moods.

Complexity

As for balance, the most striking thing in the work is the composer's use of more texturally transparent writing at significant sections: namely, in the opening, which only uses three instruments in the beginning; in the Development, which at m. 112 also uses just three instruments; in the Recapitulation, which is quite thin in texture because the inner voices are often in unison, and the ending, starting at m. 275. Only three instruments are playing at m. 289, and only two at m. 295. This is in contrast to much of the rest of the work which has denser writing such as m. 85-97, mm. 136-148, etc. Therefore, the composer begins with light texture but as he develops his material, the textures get thicker.

An interesting detail in this work is the bass pattern which changes from the opening repeated pulsating notes in the viola to m. 51, which has repeated staccato notes a fifth apart, in the cello which goes on for quite some time.

Subtlety

Although this music satisfies our expectations for the most part, there are several points where an avoidance of predictability is encountered. The introduction of harmonics at m. 194, giving a more eerie quality to the work, the tremolo intervals at m. 148 adding a certain intensity, and the parallel fifths, mentioned above. Also noteworthy are the parallel fourths at m. 140, giving an impressionistic sound to the music and lastly, the two quarter rests after the last notes with fermatas above them indicating that the composer wanted a continuing intensity even after the last note was played.

Second Movement

Stylistic Level

Sonority

The dynamic range of this piece is from *pppp* to *fortissimo*. The movement begins softly and delicately, but *forte* and *fortissimo* markings are to be found as early as m. 17. The overall dynamic range of the work is on the soft side. The entire middle section of this three-part form (starting at m. 149) and the third section (m. 240) tends to be subdued.

There is a distinct contrast in texture and dynamics between the two outer sections and the middle one. The middle section is much more static and slow moving, with long-lined melodies and a relative lack of movement in the accompanying parts.

The use of pizzicato strings creates a transparent quality which lends a sense of magic and fantasy to the music.

Harmony

Although the end of this movement suggests C major, one would be hard pressed to pinpoint specific tonal centers in this work. Most of the harmonies are ambiguous at best and seldom project a clear-cut tonality. For example, the clarinet's melody beginning at m. 51 is in G minor but this is refuted by the dissonant clash of F-sharp, C-sharp in the cello part against B-flat and C-natural in the violins, and F, G in the viola. Numerous sections like this may be found throughout the work.

Rhythm

The *Capriccio* has a regular meter of 2/4 for most of its length. Ben-Haim shifts to triple at significant places, namely when the phrases become longer and the music is more lyrical. For example, the first important place using triple meter is at mm. 165, although the clarinet, viola and second violin continue in duple meter, giving the effect of polyrhythm (two against three). Only at m. 186 do all the parts play in triple meter, and then the first violin introduces a long-lined conjunct melody. At m. 219 a significant melody, occurring exactly in the middle of the work, is played by the clarinet.

The opening tempo indication is *Molto vivo* which is maintained without interruption throughout the first section. The second section begins with *Un poco piu tranquillo*, proceeds to *Rallentando* and finally, *Ancora piu calmo*, continually moving toward a slower and slower pace. Ben-Haim never specifies a new tempo marking for the middle section; it is just felt to be considerably slower than that of the opening. This section ends with a six measure *Ritenuto* which brakes off abruptly with the return of the first section and Tempo I (*Molto vivo*).

Melody

The Capriccio begins with a fairy-like introductory idea played by the pizzicato strings. A unifying motif underlying this material is the skip of a fifth or fourth followed by a descending half-step.

Chapter Seven 137

Example 16. *2nd Movement,* mm2-3

At rehearsal letter A the clarinet enters with a long-lined melody accompanied by the introductory material. At letter B the clarinte's melody becomes more lyrical, and more sprightly with closer intervals making it more singable.

Another unifying motif which permeates the two outer sections is the four 16th-notes leading to either an 8th or a quarter-note.

Example 17. *2nd Movement,* m. 51

The middle section is in sharp contrast to the two outer ones because of the change in tempo and the legato nature of the melodic material. Here, the melodies are much longer-lined and conjunct. Indicative of this change of mood is Ben-Haim's marking in the cello part at letter F, *dolce cantando.*

At letter I, a new theme is introduced in the clarinet which closes the section and is also accompanied by counter melodies in the other instruments.

Structural Level

Clarity

There is a strong contrast to the idea with which Ben-Haim opens this work. It may be found in the second theme starting at

m. 51, where the lyrical clarinet melody is punctuated by repeated chords and rests by the supporting instruments. Except for the cello part, the other strings have a syncopated rhythm of rest-note-rest-note:

Example 18. *2nd Movement*, m. 51.

This lends a light-hearted quality to this movement.

Having a broader structure, this movement is a ternary form, the middle section of which is preceded by a 17 measure slackening of the original tempo. The return to the A section is abrupt and heralded by a *ritardando*

Proportion

The opening is organized into four-bar phrases, the middle section is not as consistent or clear-cut in phrase structure. Architecturally, this music is divided quite symmetrically. New material is introduced a quarter of the way through the work (m. 165).

The final section, which could be called a coda, marked *piu tranquillo*, is a condensation and reprise of all the material that has gone before.

The most powerful and compelling climax of the movement comes at m. 361 where a major section ends and all the instruments take part.

Chapter Seven

Integrity

The unity and coherence of this movement is accomplished through the use of the motifs mentioned above which are used throughout the work. Contrast is provided by juxtaposing the pizzicato opening with the long-lined melodies of the clarinet or strings.

The concinnity of the elements — sound, harmony, rhythm and melody, work together to produce an effect of light-heartedness balanced by tranquility. The effect of the opening pizzicato portion is quasi-pointillistic, producing a leggiero quality. Tranquility is achieved by long notes, creating a rhetorical statement of the main thematic ideas, which is especially true in the middle section.

Complexity

The most obvious contrast in this movement is between the two outer sections and the middle section. The middle section has a much slower tempo, a different meter (3/4) and longer-lined melodies. The harmonic rhythm is also slower and the texture is thinner. An interesting detail is that the return of the opening section is marked *pianissimo* in contrast to the beginning, which is merely *piano*. This section is not an exact reprise of the opening, but the style of writing suggests it, with its use of pizzicato strings creating a pointillist effect.

Another detail is the clarinet's repeated figure, beginning at m. 344,

Example 19. *2nd Movement*, m. 344

which is slurred from beginning to end. The same figure is taken up by the cello (m. 351) but here the marking is staccato throughout.

Subtlety

There is a bit of irony in the parody of an "um-pah" accompaniment to the clarinet's melody at letter B. Another touch of humor is the tossing back and forth the figure:

Example 20. *2nd Movement*, mm. 340-342.

at m. 340, which is then inverted and repeated with grim determination by the clarinet (m. 344). This is also reiterated by the cello, as mentioned above.

Third Movement

Tema Con Variazioni

Stylistic Level

Sonority

As in so many of Ben-Haim's works, much of this movement is soft and understated. It begins *piano* and ends with a *ppp* marking. The performers are obliged to project many shades of dynamics within a narrow framework. The loudest part of the work begins midway through Variation IV, which ends in a climactic out burst of *fortississimo*. This variation also has a denser texture and more subdivisions of the 3/2 meter, which prepares the listener for the powerful climax at m. 185.

Variation V, which follows, is the last variation and is strongly contrasting in dynamics to what came before, ranging only from *pianissimo* to *pianississimo*.

Harmony

Although the third movement of this work is marked *Tema Con Variazioni*, and starts in A major and ends in A major with an added sixth, this piece cannot be clearly described as tonal because there are too many sections that have no tonal center. The opening of the theme in parallel fourths and fifths is reminiscent of organum, with slowly moving half notes in triple meter and the melismatic clarinet melody above. This goes on until m. 9 when the cello begins a melody which is in imitative counterpoint with the clarinet part. The harmonic "color" thus produced creates a mood of gentle longing.

The first variation looks as though it should be in either A major or A minor by the very extended pedal on A in the cello part, going from mm. 22 through 27, but the E-flat and B-flat in the descending scale imply a transposed Aeolian scale in the key of G. The variation ends in F major, is contrapuntal in texture and also has elements of imitation in it, as shown at mm. 42-44. Variation 2 has no tonal center. Harmonic tension is created through the use of dissonant, cluster-like chords which, together with the melody, are quite chromatic. Tension is also enhanced with the melody, are quite chromatic. Tension is also enhanced by the use of staccatissimo, and occasionally pizzicato and arco bowings are used simultaneously to play the staccatissimo quarter notes. (mm. 55-57). The almost constant chromaticism of this music gives the effect of wandering through different harmonies. Although Variation 3 starts with a linear style of writing, at m. 100 there is a change to an arpeggiated style of writing in the cello part with a slower melody on top. Similar material to the beginning returns at m. 113 and this variation ends in D minor with an added G- sharp in the clarinet.

Variation 4, which is more sprightly than the others, features unison writing, a favorite technique of Ben-Haim's. Within this heterophonic style, the composer chooses to write an Arabic-sounding melody. This is accomplished by close intervalic writing, most being major or minor seconds, combined with many repeated notes, and turns such as found in m. 125. The melody is then played much more quickly starting at m. 131, marked *Allegro*. At m. 137 there is a change to more chordal writing, with alternating parallel fifths in the two lower instruments. This accompanies the melody which becomes louder and more frenzied, continuing to the end of the variation and ending in C major.

Variation 5 is the exact opposite of what came before in many ways. It is much less dense with many rests in the strings, much longer notes and a return to the organum-like chordal writing of the beginning, with long notes underlying a more florid melody on top. There is much parallel major and minor writing, producing interesting harmonic colors. An example may be found at m. 206, which clearly ends in A major with an added 6th.

Rhythm

The meter is almost completely regular in this movement except for the contrasting 6/4 marking at m. 178 to the end, which tends to elongate the phrases. Although the meter is quite regular, there is an impressive array of rhythmic devices which are used to vary and add interest to the music. An example is the opening, with its slow organum-like parallel fourths and fifths, under a more quickly moving melody. In Variation 1, rhythmic foreshortening occurs, where Ben-Haim uses half notes, quarters, triplet quarters and finally eighths to achieve the effect of a written-out accelerando.

Rhythmically, Variation 2 recalls the scherzando mood of the previous movement. Although this time it is slower and marked *Molto grazzioso*. The primitive rhythm consists mainly of many repeated quarter notes in all instruments, sometimes interspersed with eighth notes (m. 50). This is expanded upon with more eighth notes (m. 56-57), and the quarters are embellished with grace-notes starting at m. 54.

Variation 3, marked *piu calmo* has an interesting effect in that the three notes written in the second violin part:

Example 21. *3rd Movement,* m. 90

which would normally fall into a triplet pattern, are written in roups of four, thereby giving each note in its turn an accent on the first beat at the appropriate point. Of the three variations discussed thus far, it is the first one which is rhythmically closest to the Theme.

With its melody, variation 4 is ancient sounding, which is a frequent device of Ben-Haim's especially when he is introducing climactic sections. Here the closeness of the intervals as well as the repetitive rhythms:

Example 22. *3rd Movement*, mm. 120-121.

suggests the Middle Eastern quarter-tone sound. The section at m. 126-130 is rather primitive-sounding with quarter notes underneath a quicker moving melody in the clarinet part. The alternating fifths punctuated by rests in the lower two instruments starting at m. 136 are an interesting rhythmic device in a contrast to what came before.

There are many tempo changes in this variation, which starts out *Allegretto, poco a poco accelerando,* reaching *Piu Allegro* at m. 163 and continuing through another *accelerando* to a brilliant ending marked *Con fuoco.* This rhythmic device of starting slowly and getting faster and faster is characteristic of Gypsy music.

The last variation, marked *Adagio assai e misterioso* is a return to the opening theme in the same key but with a much thinner rhythmic and harmonic background.

Melody

An outstanding feature of the clarinet melody is the repeated long notes followed by quarters and eighths, using mainly small intervals.

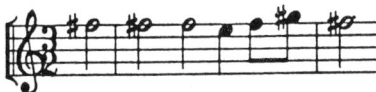

Example 23. *Tema,* mm. 1-3

The melody is mainly organized into four-bar phrases with the second half having the largest interval, a downward skip of an octave. There is also melodic imitation between the instruments, notably at m. 8 and then occurring in the cello, starting at m. 10.

Variation 1 has a rhythmic elongation of the melody in the first violin part at m. 26.

Variation 2 is a diminution of the melody; it is there, but with shorter note values and not in its entirety. This variation is notable for its chromatic treatment of the melodic material, for example m. 53. There is an augmentation of the melody in Variation 3 at mm. 99-107 in the clarinet part and a diminution in the first violin part.

The shorter note values of the melody are expanded upon in Variation 4. This features melodic writing and has a Middle Eastern sonority, produced by a combination of turns and closely repeated seconds on consecutive notes. Keeping in mind the balance of ancient and contemporary sounds in this music, the two *sforzandi* at m. 156 might represent a tambourine flourish. Although the melody at m. 157 sounds like the beginning on first hearing, it is a rhythmically more intricate version of the opening.

The final variation is an extreme contrast to the previous material. The haunting opening theme is heard again, this time marked *misterioso.* An interesting detail is that this time, in mm. 183-185, the first note of the four eighths in the melody is C-natural, where it was a C-sharp in the beginning (m.3), indicating that the key is now a minor.

Structural Level

Clarity

Although there is symmetry in this theme, which is binary with a short codetta at m. 20, the variations are not all so well balanced. Certain elements of the theme are expanded upon during the course of the variations, which lead to an asymmetrical design in some of them. For example, in Variation II, the repeated-note idea from the Theme (mm. 1-2), is extensively developed for five measures (mm. 48-52).

It is from Variation III onwards that the texture increases in density as well as rhythmic complexity. Variation V, in contrast to this flurry of activity, is stripped down to its most basic elements. The opening melody returns in the same key, balanced by transparent string accompaniment and frequent rests.

Proportion

In this movement, the composer deviates from his characteristic symmetrical style. There are some instances of proportional writing, such as the Theme, as well as Variation 1 and the final Variation. Although the inner variations are longer, the fourth is the longest (60 measures). When one carefully observes the tempo markings, every variation requires a slow tempo except the fourth, which is marked *Allegretto, poco a poco accelerando*. This means that in actual playing time, it is no longer than the others.

There is an interesting spot halfway through the piece, starting at m. 99, where there is a combination of the melody in augmented form in the second violin and viola and diminished form in the first violin. The arpeggiated bass with a sonorous lyrical melody in the clarinet is a romantic touch. Although lyrical in nature, it has a rather primitive sonority.

The most intense climax of this piece comes nearly at the end right before the last variation at m. 180.

Compared to the other variations in this movement, this is by far dramatic and tempestuous in character.

Integrity

One thematic idea runs throughout this work and binds it together. It is also bound together by the slow chordal accompaniment alternating with imitative contrapuntal techniques. Often the slow chords are built up of fifths and fourths, which help to balance the work. The undulating nocturne-like accompaniment found at m. 99 is in contrast to the stately opening. Often dissonant, at times nebulous harmonies and chords give way to the determined nature of the fourth variation.

Complexity

Texturally, there is a clear contrast in this movement between the inner variations and the outer ones. The beginning Theme and the ending Variation V are simpler and more transparent in character and are in direct contrast to the inner sections. They are also more complex rhythmically and dynamically.

Although Ben-Haim uses only one theme throughout the work, contrast is achieved through the use of rhythmical intricacies such as the arpeggiated figure in the middle movement mentioned above, as well as dance-like and primitive rhythms found in Variation IV. The extremely chromatic treatment of the melodic material in Variation II is another device the composer uses to achieve a balanced design. He also mixes primitive material such as parallel fifths and fourths together with dissonant writing which contrasts with consonant sounds.

Subtlety

The harmonics used are an example of an otherworldly sound starting at m. 73. The use of the word *flautando* (like a flute) is curious except when the performer realizes that the composer wanted to have the low sounds executed distinctly.

Notes

1. Jehoash Hirshberg, *Paul Ben-Haim, His Life and Works.* (Tel Aviv: Am Oved Publishers, 1989).

150 — The Music of Paul Ben-Haim

First Movement (continued)

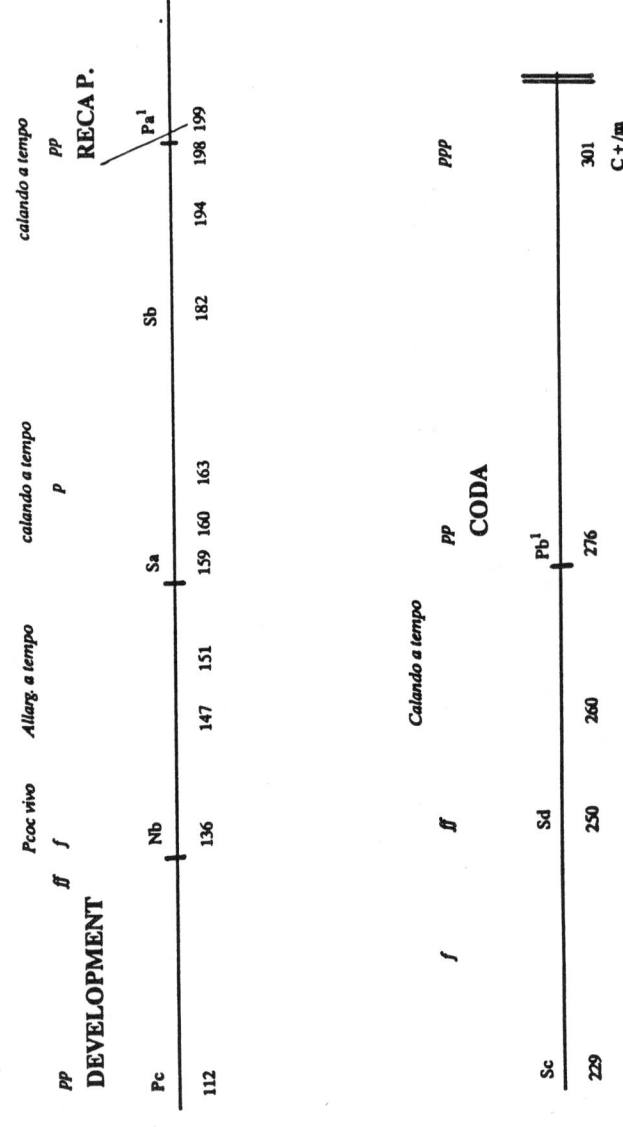

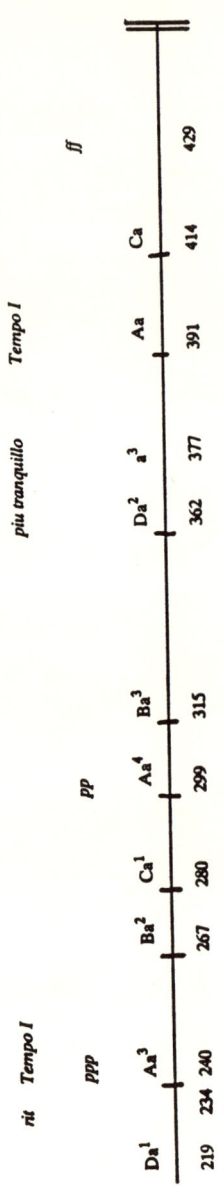

Quintet. Second Movement (continued)

Chapter Seven

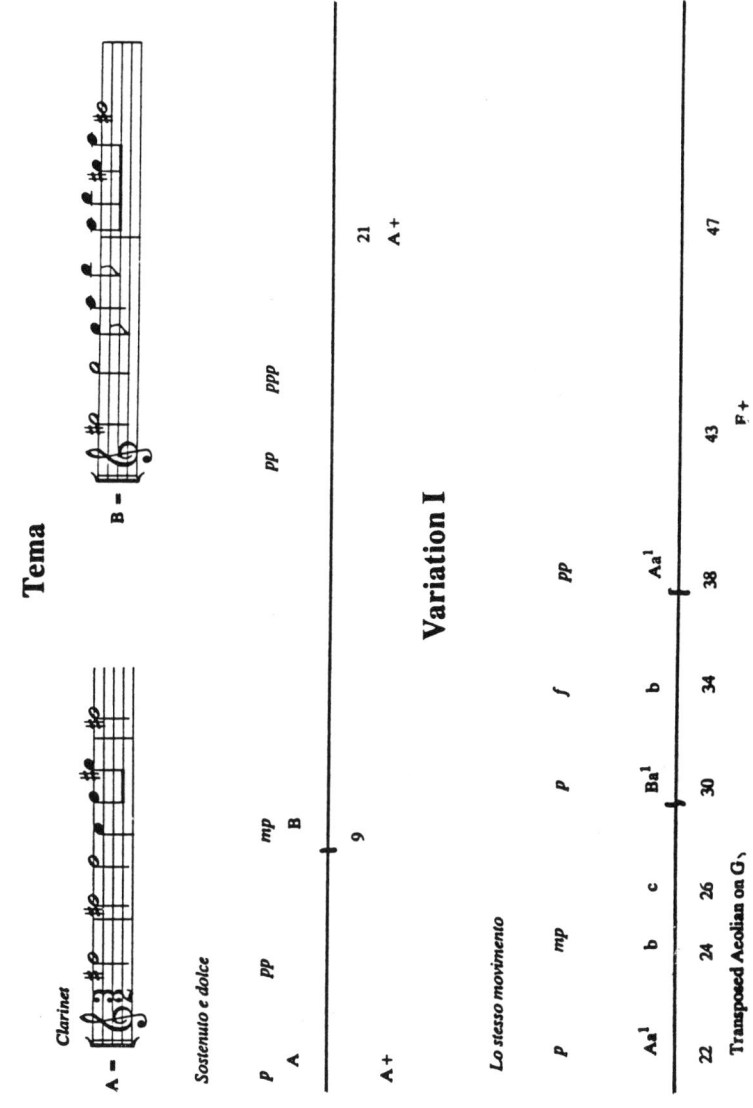

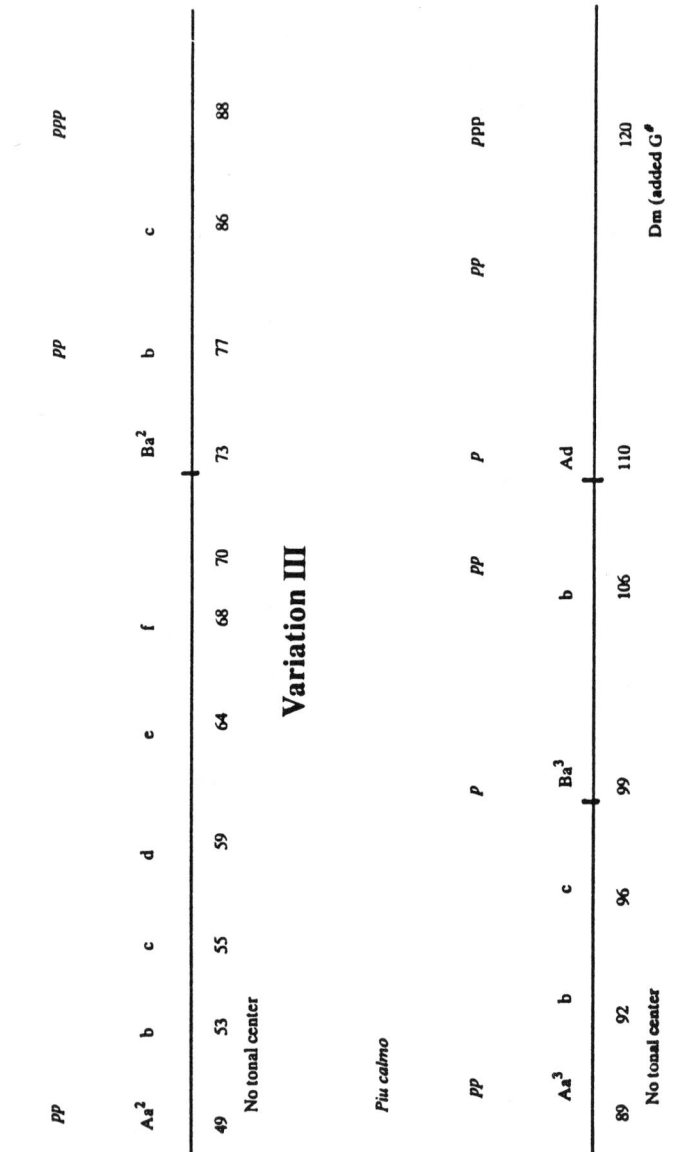

Chapter Seven 155

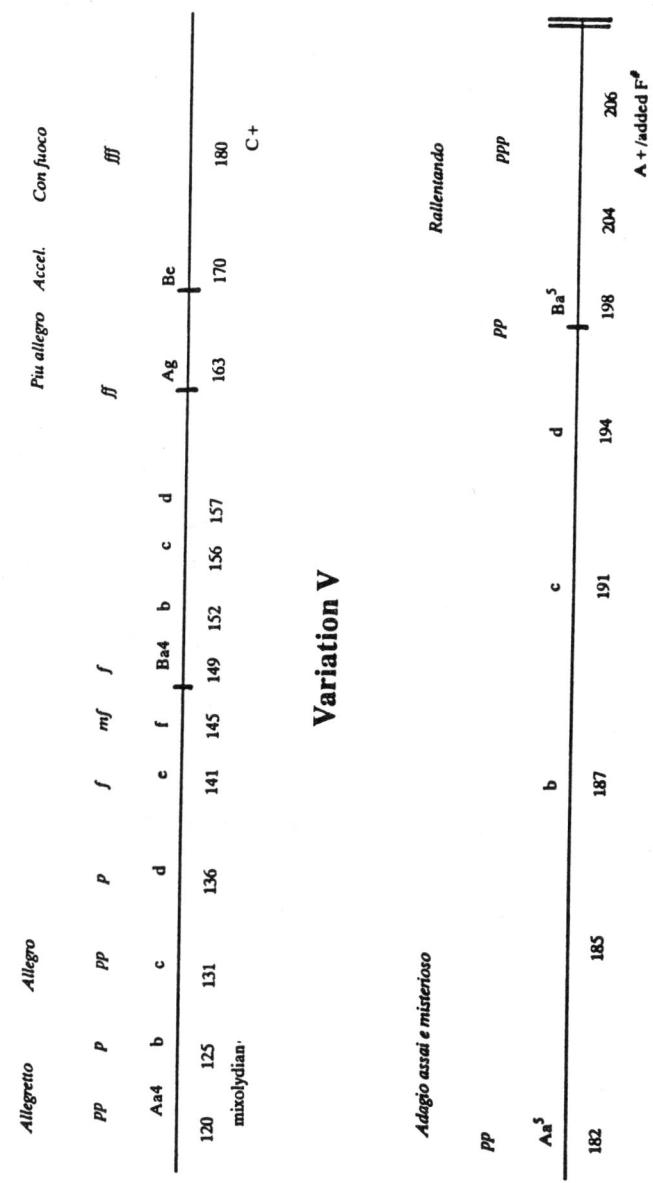

Chapter Eight

SONATA IN G FOR VIOLIN SOLO

1951

Paul Ben-Haim's Solo Sonata, composed in Tel-Aviv in the autumn of 1951 and dedicated to Yehudi Menuhin, is among his most personal and forceful works. Its three movements are simple in form and poignant in content, with the *Allegro energico* combining the form of a prelude with the drive of a toccata; the *Lento e soto voce,* played *con sordino* throughout, is an expressive fantasy of "Mediterranean music" and, though the composer asks it to be played "without colour," it produces a strangely attractive instrumental coloring by employing grace notes trills, and echo effects; the *Molto allegro* returns with the drive and force of the opening movement with *hora* rhythms faintly discernible in the rhythmic texture.

The Sonata was first performed by Yehudi Menuhin in Carnegie Hall, New York, on 4 February, 1952; the same artist gave the Israeli premiere of the work in April of that year.

Stylistic Level

Sonority

Although written for solo violin, the movement is characterized by great intensity beginning *forte* and ending *fortissimo*. Between these extremes are moments of delicacy and mystery, such as the harmonic marked *ppp* at m. 52, which is also the end of a complete section.

Allegro energico suggests a piece of great strength and endurance, but there is contrast in sections by the use of the word *Pesante* at mm. 5, 8 and 10, balanced with a *Poco sostenuto* sound at m. 14. Within the *Poco sostenuto* many instances of *pianissimo* and *leggiero* may be found. At *Tempo guisto*, m. 44, the same effect is repeated; there is a *poco sostenuto* marking at m.47, immediately followed by *forte-piano* at m. 48, producing uncharacteristic dynamic extremes. This leads into a passage in an extremely high register (m. 51), marked *flautando* (like a flute), and climaxing in harmonics at m. 52, marked *ppp*.

At m. 59, where the main theme returns again, phrases begin with four-note chords, increasing the depth of the sonority. At m. 66, there is a reprise of the opening; the theme is introduced in the middle register and then repeated an octave higher. Then in a flourish of downward cascading 16th-notes, the movement comes to a dramatic close.

Harmony

This is a work which the performer can be sure is in the key of G. Ben-Haim strongly establishes G with the tonic and leading-tone comprising the first few notes but immediately writes an F-natural. In m. 2 there is a constant interweaving of the G, F-sharp, G, F-natural and this extremely chromatic movement is found in most measures, except in places such as mm. 36-39, which are more chordal in structure. These interweaving, chromatic ambiguities immediately recall the quarter-tone, which is characteristic of Middle Eastern and especially Arabic music. The composer often moves in and out of various harmonies, but eventually returns to the key of G.

Rhythm

There are many meter changes in this movement, although some, (6/4 changing to 3/4), are more significant than others. The important changes, such as at mm. 24, 28, 31, etc., add a quality of suppleness and unpredictability which is typical of Middle Eastern music. This is one of many elements which create an exotic, otherworldly aura in this work.

The 7/4 meter comes at a moment where there is a return of the opening theme at m. 26. These changing meters often aid in the expansion of an existing motif.

There are many places where *ritenuto* and *a tempo* are indicated, often coming at ends or beginning of phrases.

Melody

This movement has the forward propulsion and drive of a toccata together with the free-flowing style of a prelude. The melody is conjunct with many chromatic intervals, typical of the land which inspired it. The first phrase group may be considered extending from mm. 1 through 6, with the next phrase beginning at m. 7.

In contrast to the beginning, the melody is at times diatonic and disjunct, for example m. 32 through 44 where it becomes widely spaced broken chords, in typical violin style.

When the composer wants more intensity, he repeats the opening theme in ever higher registers. At m. 1 it appears in the key of G, at m. 16 in C and finally at the climactic highest point at m. 26 in A. Because Ben-Haim avoids the qualifying 3rd, it is impossible to determine whether the mode is major or minor.

Structural Level

Clarity

The first movement is not in sonata form, but is an elaboration and expansion upon the opening motif:

Example 24. *1st Movement*, m. 1.

which is a unifying device for the entire piece. At m. 32, a new idea is introduced consisting of a dotted 8th followed by 16ths, but this is not developed to any great extent. This idea leads into the one episode in the movement (m. 42) which is markedly different, being made up of 8ths and quarters and is in a much higher register than the piece has been thus far. There is also a *ritenuto* mark which, coupled with *molto espr.*, which makes for a striking change of tempo.

Proportion

Unlike many of Ben-Haim's works, the treatment of the phrase structure of this piece is quite asymmetrical. For example the first phrase is just five measures long; the next two are one measure each. At m. 19 there is a phrase of seven measures' duration.

However, the large sections of the piece are nearly symmetrical, and only off by a measure or two, which retains the improvisatory style. For example the first large section is 16 measures long. It is followed by a smaller one of 10 measures; this is in turn balanced by a 15 measure section.

The two main ideas in this movement consist of the chromatic, conjunct opening melody and the more disjunct, diatonic motif which begins slightly before the middle of the piece, at m. 32.

Integrity

The unity of this movement is a result of the strongly stated chromatic idea running throughout the work. There is also balance achieved by introducing the opening material and then expanding upon it, for example at m. 9. Also, after the whole movement has run its course, the opening material is recalled in the last few measures which insures that the motivic unity is kept intact.

The concinnity of the elements within sections mainly held together by the coordination of the melody with the rhythm. The melody, close-knit and spun out, is balanced by the rhythm which is quite irregular, being broken up by meter changes as well as changes in tempo.

Complexity

At the main climax of the movement at m. 42, Ben-Haim provides great contrast with sudden simplicity of melody and rhythm, compared to the agitation which permeates much of the previous material. In addition, the disjunct melody starting at m. 32 moves rhythmically and melodically with more uniform regularity than what came before.

Even in the contrasting sections, the atmosphere is one of determination and strength.

Subtlety

There are several instances of deviation from convention. The 7/4 meter which occurs once in the movement at m. 26, is an example of creating intensity through the use of irregular and unusual meters. Other striking effects are the climax at m. 42, which is outstanding in its simplicity, and the one at m. 52, marked *ppp*. The impact of this effect is heightened by the use of harmonics.

Second Movement

Stylistic Level

Sonority

Dynamically, this movement is in direct contrast to the first movement. Except for four places, the entire movement is pervaded not only with a soft dynamic level ranging from *mezzo piano* to *pianississimo* (*ppp*), but *sordino* is indicated in the opening, literally calling for a muted sound. The opening indication, *Lento e sotto voce*, enhances this subdued and mysterious quality. The direction, *senza colore* asks the performer to play without color, but this produces a strangely attractive sound by employing grace notes, trills and echo effects.

The climax of the work occurs at mm. 13-14. One of the few *mezzo forte* and *forte* measures, it is also a reiteration and variation of the opening theme. It is placed an octave higher, a registration change bringing heightened intensity of sound and emotion. At the other end of the spectrum, the end of the first idea at m. 8 ends *ppp*. The other two places where there are *mezzo forte* markings is at mm. 17 and 18, but only for the first few notes of the passage. Each of these phrases fades off into *pianissimo*.

The sound becomes denser in the middle section of the opening starting at m. 9 and culminates at m. 13 in the climax, which is marked *molto espressivo e cantabile*. There is also a cadenza-like treatment starting at m. 20 and continuing nearly to the end, with 32nd and 64th-note runs. However, this section is governed by the marking *Piu calmo*, which discourages any virtuoso display and enhances the longer lines of the melodic ideas.

Harmony

The opening motif uses the Aeolian mode transposed to F, and this device is used extensively through the work, but the tonality of the movement is obscure. It obviously involves the note C, but it is unclear whether the reference is to C major or C minor. The ending is nebulous because the last sound heard is an open fifth, C and G.

This movement has a mysterious and exotic aura due to the use of modality and its ambiguous tonalities.

Rhythm

There is an abundance of rhythmic variety in this movement, as evidenced by frequent meter changes and unusual beat groups such as 7/4. The opening 5 measures contain the following meters: 7/4, 6/4, 7/4, 6/4, 7/4.

This almost constantly changing meter adds a distinctive Mediterranean flavor and enhances the dreamy quality of the music.

An important feature of the rhythmic design of the opening motif is the use of double dotted 8ths going to 32nds:

Example 25. *2nd Movement*, m. 1.

The opening is marked *Lento e soto voce* in keeping with the subtle flavor created. At the climax, mm. 13-14, there is the marking, *molto espressivo e cantabile*, which denotes Ben-Haim's desire for a broadening of the tempo. This movement has less of a feeling of perpetual motion than the previous one, because often at the beginnings and endings of phrases there are rests which provide repose.

Melody

There are two main themes in the movement. The first is in m. 1 and the other at m. 9, both being cantabile and conjunct. They both employ dotted rhythms in different ways and throughout the work there are embellishments such as grace-notes, trills and echo effects, as mentioned above.

The opening idea is greatly expanded upon through the use of cadenza-like runs using 32nd and 64th notes. Also most of the runs in the first half of the piece are ascending and in the second half they are descending. When Tempo I returns at m. 21 it is a significant point because the melody is an almost exact inversion of m. 9.

The phrase structure is irregular. For example the first phrase is 8 measures long and the second at m. 9 is 6 measures.

Structural Level

Clarity

The second movement is organized into three basic sections, mm 1-12 comprising the first and m. 13-19, the second, which is in a higher register. The third section begins at m. 21, marked Tempo I.

This intense and meditative movement is unified by the dotted rhythm in m. 1.

There is a relationship to the first movement in that both use a motif containing a descending second.

Example 26. *1st Movement*, m. 1.

Example 27. *2nd Movement*, m. 1.

At *piu calmo* the motif is finally abandoned and new material is introduced which brings the movement to a quiet close.

Proportion

This work is 25 measures long and the main climax occurs almost exactly half way through at m. 13. Eight measures later at m. 21 is the final important section.

Three quarters through at m. 20 is where the composer writes with total abandon, letting fantasy dictate his rhythmic, harmonic and melodic inspiration.

Integrity

This piece is unified through the use of the opening idea: a double-dotted 8th going to a 64th note. This is repeated three times and ends with a quarter note. The second theme (m. 9) balances this idea with a dotted 8th going to two 32nds. The elaboration of both ideas harmonically, melodically and rhythmically is consistent throughout the work. It also binds the piece together motivically.

A masterful touch is achieved with the use of clipped dotted rhythms followed by elongated, improvisatory declamations. The concinnity of the elements is also interrelated with the use of conjunct melody and frequent embellishments; irregular, repetitious rhythms and a harmonic scheme based on the Aeolian mode. These all work together to produce a meditative and rhapsodic statement.

Complexity

In relation to the entire work, the first and second themes represent a strong contrast. The primary theme with its dotted rhythms is abrupt, repetitious and exotic; the second theme at m. 9, is more lyrical with a longer legato line.

Starting at m. 17 the opening idea is expanded upon with more widely spaced intervals.

Subtlety

There are several subtle touches which are outstanding in this second movement. The trills, grace-notes and echo effects are devices to enhance the melody as well as the use of glissandi at mm. 7 and 13. The use of harmonics at the end helps to create an otherworldly quality.

Third Movement

Stylistic Level

Sonority

Although this movement starts out on a subdued level there are three places which are climactic points and they are articulated by dynamic marking of *forte* and *fortissimo*. The first climax which is at the end of a significant section is m. 43. The next occurs at m. 87 which is just prior to *diminuendo poco a poco*. Before returning to the opening at m. 98, marked piano, the music builds again to the end of the piece, where the last note is marked *sfff*.

At the end of the first climax, m. 43, there is a rise in the registration ending with a *fortissimo* marking. At the next climax (m. 87), the texture is much denser and there many double stops.

The general quality of sound in the movement can be characterized by the word *pesante*, which Ben-Haim uses throughout the piece. It should also be noted that part of the opening indication includes the words *senza sordino*.

Harmony

This movement ends in G, which relates back to the first movement. There is a significant detail between the first two notes, the tritone, G and D-flat which plays an important role in the movement. Almost every time the main *hora* theme is restated, it appears.

For the most part, this piece is in some form of G.

There is also frequent use of the Oriental-sounding augmented 2nd, for example, at mm. 11, 29 and 41. Because of chromatic runs and seemingly unrelated scales, it seems as though the tonality gets further away from the key of G, but in the end Ben-Haim seems to imply a return to G through the use of a G pedal-point.

Rhythm

This is a piece of great forward propulsion and should be played with the same driving force as the opening movement, and with *hora* rhythms discernible in the rhythmic texture. However, before nearly every return of the opening theme, there is a slower section preceding it.

The meter of this movement is much more regular than is the previous one, and when it does change, it goes from quadruple to duple meter, 4/4 to 6/4, which is fundamentally no change at all, but only serves to elongate a phrase.

This piece is marked *Molto allegro*, and should be interpreted as an example of the national dance of Israel, the *hora*. It is made up of an 8th, four 16ths and an 8th. Then there is a contrasting section first heard at m. 23 consisting of quarter notes followed by 8th notes and then 8th rests. This idea which is expanded upon returns three times and disrupts the feeling of perpetual motion.

It is also used to bring the piece to a close immediately after a frenzied upward rushing chromatic run in open 5ths.

Melody

This piece is built on two musical ideas, the first in *hora* rhythm, using a tritone and a conjunct melody and the other, a slower interlude in 8th notes, consisting of large leaps, as mentioned above. The second idea is unmistakable because it contrasts so dramatically with the first.

The first melodic climax comes at m. 43, the second at 78 and the third at m. 108. These are the culmination of cadenza-like runs growing out of the *hora* idea.

Structural Level

Clarity

The main motif of the 3rd movement is also related to the first:

Example 28. *3rd Movement,* m. 1.

Example 29. *1st Movement,* m. 1.

This motif also unifies this movement in the same manner as the other two.

The toccata-like perpetual motion character of the work is interrupted periodically by episodes at mm. 23-28, mm. 43-62 and mm. 78-98. These divide the movement into three sections.

The first movement is not in sonata form, but is in free style and is an elaboration and expansion upon the opening motif.

At m. 32, a new idea is introduced consisting of a dotted 8th followed by 16ths, but this is not developed to any great extent. At m. 43 there is a *ritenuto* mark which, coupled with *molto espressivo,* makes for a striking change of tempo.

Proportion

In terms of proportion in the large context, the architecture of this piece is not symmetrical. The first section is 23 measures long, the next (mm. 23-43) is 20 measures and the next 16 measures (mm. 62-78).

Unlike the first movement, this work is much less balanced in the length of its principal sections. However, its structure is more complex and less improvisatory than the second movement.

Integrity

Unity and coherance are achieved with balanced contrast between the first idea and the second, m. 23. Also an interweaving of rhythmic, dynamic and melodic elements produce tension and release throughout the work which provide unity and smooth transitions throughout.

The way the movement develops is organic as one section flows into the next through the use of cascading, cadenza-like extensions. Because of the placement of the rests in the second idea at m. 23, the forward motion is arrested. However, there is a forceful momentum which ends with a crashing eruption of determination.

Complexity

Looking at the work as a whole, the first and second ideas provide great contrast. The first is the more lyrical of the two, being more conjunct, although it is choppy to a certain extent, it is song-like and legato than the other idea.

The second idea is simpler in design than the opening, but Ben-Haim has taken these two distinctly different themes and has woven them into a work of vivid power.

Subtlety

The second idea is a surprise because it abruptly stops the forward motion of the piece. The use at the end of the ascending chromatic open fifths at m. 107 produces an air of wild abandon and is contrasted directly with the *molto rit.* section immediately following which has chords and rests.

Chapter Eight

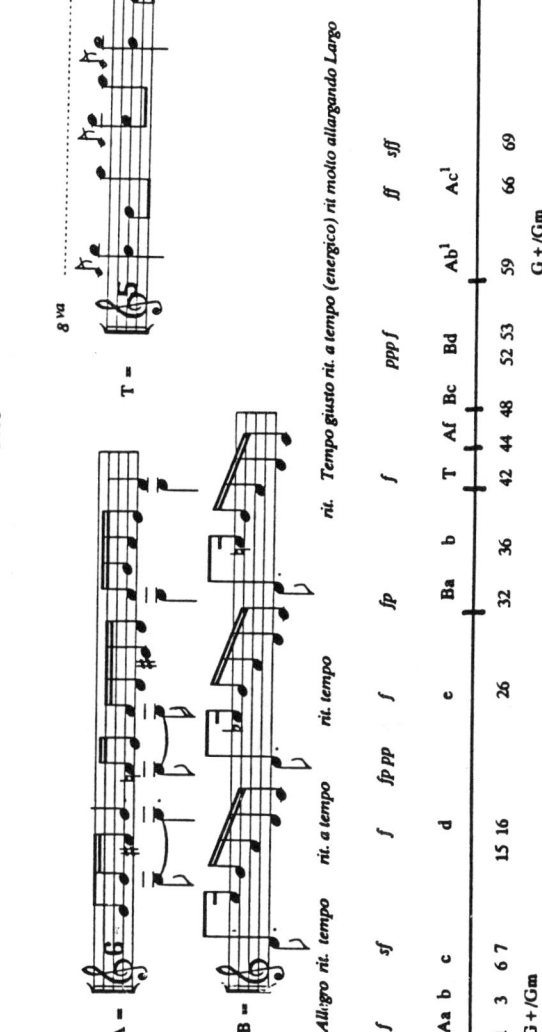

Sonata in G. Second Movement

Chapter Eight

Sonata in G. Third Movement

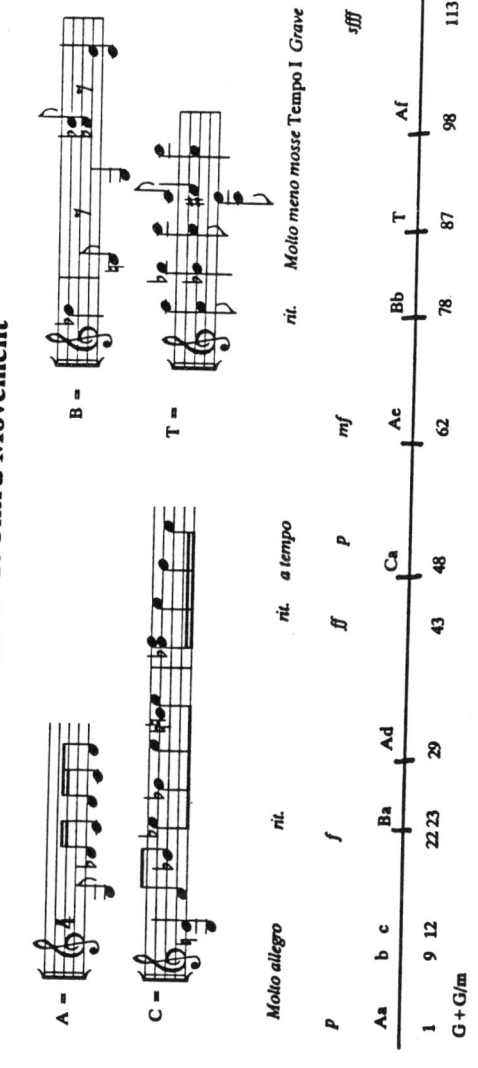

Chapter Nine

SERENADE

For Flute And String Trio

1952

Serenade for flute and string trio, recorded by Aurèle Nicolet and members of the Israeli String Quartet in 1967, is a colorful piece of twelve minutes duration. It has three movements, the second and third of which follow each other without a break.

First Movement

Stylistic Level

Sonority

The sound of the flute dominates the whole movement because it is in a higher register and the accompanying strings play more of a supporting role. There is only one place where the flute drops out for a long period of time, starting at m. 38 until 49, where the other instruments provide contrapuntal dialogue. There are only a few places where the strings dominate melodically; one of these is at m. 57, where the viola states the Second Theme. Another is the Recapitulation (m. 92), where the cello nstead of the flute, announces the Principal theme, and at m. 121 where the cello has the Second Theme.

The main climactic section starts building at the *mezzo forte* in m. 83 and doesn't diminish until m. 90, where there is a *diminuendo* indicated. Marked *agitatio,* it is the most powerful in the movement, and prepares for the Recapitulation. Preceding this, a lesser climax takes place starting m. 47, culminating at m. 51; it is short-lived and paves the way for the Second Theme.

The dynamics of this first movement range from *ppp* to *forte.*

Harmony

The Principal Theme, introduced by the flute is based on the G natural minor scale, which is the transposed Aeolian mode. At m. 51 the first section clearly ends in C, but whether major or minor is impossible to determine. The Second Theme, starting at m. 52, begins in B-flat minor.

There is a contrasting contrapuntal section starting at m. 39, involving the strings with the flute tacit. This is unique in that there is no other part of the movement having scale-wise, imitative counterpoint.

Rhythm

This movement has a few meter changes, (mm. 4, 5, 20 and 21) near the beginning and at the end, but otherwise triple meter prevails. Except for a short introduction in the strings consisting of three quarter notes, the Principal Theme played by the flute contains a motif which unifies the whole work:

Example 30. *1st Movement*, m. 2.

The rest which precedes the two 16ths is an important element in this motif because it is nearly always present.

The Second Theme, starting at m. 52 is more relaxed, starting on a dotted quarter and has a rest at the end of the measure rather than at the beginning. Here the phrase is six bars long as contrasted with the Principal Theme's four-bar phrase.

Aside from several *ritardandos,* the only real tempo change comes near the end of the movement, where m. 139 is marked *piu lento.* Ben-Haim consistently uses 16th-note runs at the climactic moments in the movement.

Melody

There are two main themes dominating this work, the Principal Theme and the Second Theme which begins at m. 52 on D-flat, a tritone below the opening on G. The Second Theme's first three notes are melodically the similar to the opening; rhythmically they are not the same, however.

The introductory four notes in the strings anticipate the shape of both the First and Second Themes. These four notes always precede the statement of the First Theme, although they don't always have the same melodic shape.

Example 31. *1st Movement,* m. 1.

The opening starts out with a four-bar phrase, which is followed by one of five bars, showing an irregular phrase structure.

Except for the main climax at m. 85, the registration is mostly in the medium range.

Structural Level

Clarity

The first movement of the Serenade is a clear-cut example of sonata form. The Exposition comprises the first 69 measures, the Development runs from m. 70 to m. 92, and the Coda begins at m. 140. Within these large areas, there is the First Theme in the Exposition, which begins at m. 2. The Second Theme is clearly prepared for with two beats of silence after the movement's first strong climax.

The beginning of the Development is heralded by the first tempo change in the movement, marked, *Ritenuto*. The spot is also marked "*pp*" which is the softest dynamic marking thus far. The stormy Development ends with a still more drastic tempo change, *Molto ritardando*, the flute's last note being extended with a fermata. The Recapitulation begins with a statement of the Principal Theme in the cello instead of the flute.

The Coda is marked *Piu Lento* with the flute's motif skipping down a 9th rather than the more frequent 2nd. One last plaintive reiteration of the motif occurs in the violin part at m. 144.

Proportion

Structurally, the large sections of this movement are quite cohesive. The entire movement consists of 151 measures; significant structural segments may be found roughly every 50 measures. The most intense climax occurs at m. 85, a little beyond the halfway point. A lesser climax (mm. 49-51) happens a third of the way through. All these climaxes have their logical and inevitable place in the structural matrix of the movement.

Integrity

Motivically this piece is carefully integrated by individual elements and is in fact a result of Ben-Haim's skillful handling of compositional technique. The macrodynamic areas occur at structurally significant places. The *fortissimo* and *forte* markings and the rhythmic unity are balanced by the composer's use of modal harmonic writing balanced by contrapuntal movement (mm. 39-49).

Rhythmically, the First and Second Themes contrast each other through the use of faster moving opening note values, as compared to the longer-lined Second Theme. The entire movement is unified with a motif which is similar in the First and Second Themes.

The composer synthesizes the formal musical elements into a cohesive and compelling design.

Complexity

The simplicity of this work lies in the fact that the flute part dominates almost the entire first movement, with the string parts being mainly supportive.

Its complexity stems from the fact that there are varying degrees of contrast within the work. For example, the balancing of the chordal accompaniment pattern as opposed to the contrapuntal, almost "walking bass" style, as well as the similarities yet distinct differences between the First and Second Themes. Contrast is also achieved through the frequent change of meter in the beginning as compared to the more subtle regular meter which prevails for the larger part of the work, m. 50 to the end of the movement.

Subtlety

There are three places (mm. 42, 44 and 46) where 5/4 meter occurs and presents an interesting contrast with the more common 3/4 and 4/4 meters. Another detail is the use of *forte* with the word *subito* several times in succession starting at m. 116.

There are several special effects for the violinist which create a variety of unusual sounds. At m. 70, *punta d'arco* (end of the bow), which produces a thin, eerie sound; at m. 86, *au talon* (near the frog), indicating a harsh, grating effect; and at m. 115, *sul tasto* (on the fingerboard), which produces a delicate, transparent tone. From mm. 103 to 114, the violin has harmonics, which adds a particularly striking effect.

Second Movement

Stylistic Level

Sonority

For the most part, this movement requires a subdued and delicate sound. The word *dolce* is used many times throughout the work in the various parts. The dynamics range from *pianissimo* to *fortissimo* and the climax in fact begins at m. 62 and ends at m. 77 with the marking *sempre fortissimo*.

The composer is quite explicit in his directions and often indicates *con sordino* (with mute) or *senza sordino* (without mute); an example of this is mm. 17, 18 and 21. He also indicates *senza vibrato* at m. 24 and then right before the return of *Tempo I* at m. 91, m. 90 is marked *con sordino*, showing that he wanted a muted and reserved repetition of the opening. The last measure has the words *senza sordino*, while the penultimate measure is marked *morendo*. This is because Ben-Haim begins the last movement without a break. He wishes to have more sound to lead into the final movement.

Exactly at the point of the climax, mm. 63 through 79 the texture is thickest compared to the rest of the piece. When the opening section returns at m. 91 it is one octave lower and should be played with darker colors than at the opening.

The middle section, marked *allegretto,* has several *scherzando* markings, indicating a much more lighthearted, humorous character than the sections which begin and end the piece.

Harmony

This piece ends in F-sharp major but it doesn't bear any relation to the key signature of four sharps. Although there are areas with well-defined tonal centers throughout the work, one cannot point to this or that place and determine with certainty which key it is in.

There are sections where a pedal-point is used such as m. 3, where a sustained F-sharp is played by the cello for several measures, and then again at m. 11. An interrupted B in the cello part is another example, beginning at m. 24 and continues with a few variants until m. 51. There is also a trilled pedal on the note C at m. 83, and one on D-sharp continuing from mm. 91 to 94.

Texturally, the *Allegretto* middle section is quite contrapuntal, with the flute and upper strings engaging in an extensive dialogue.

Rhythm

This movement is marked *Tranquillamente improvisando* and is divided into distinct sections. The opening is like a recitative and serves as an introduction to the *Allegretto leggieramente mosso.* Ben-Haim has marked the viola *solo dolce rubato* in keeping with style. The improvisatory nature of this opening is further enhanced by the meter changes. Except for the beginning and the end, the meter is regular throughout the work, being either 3/4 or 3/8.

The end of the *Allegretto* section is marked *Tempo I* and returns to the same material as the introduction, but includes *recitativo* parts extended by *accellerandos* and 32nd-notes.

There is a rhythmic parallel with the first movement in that they both have meter changes in the beginning and ending sections, while the longer middle sections do not.

Melody

Melodically, in the opening *recitativo* there is a dialogue between the viola and flute parts. Later the cello also has a statement starting m. 18.

Beginning with the *Allegretto* section, there is a more structured melody marked *scherzando*, consisting of four-bar phrases and supported by the cello's pedal on B. At m. 42, the violin imitates the flute's part, and at m. 53 the viola has the same melody in an inverted form.

At m. 91 the introductory material returns in slightly altered form an octave lower, and at m. 100, the scherzando idea is briefly recalled.

Structural Level

Clarity

This movement is obviously ABA ternary form. Although the middle section is longer in terms of numbers of measures, it actually takes less time to play than the outer sections. The metronome marking for the opening *Tranquillamente* is 40 to a quarter-note, while the *Allegretto* section is 60 to a dotted quarter-note. With its imitative counterpoint, the middle section is much more strictly organized than the opening, which is improvisatory in nature and has the declamatory style of a recitative.

Proportion

This movement is more symmetrical than the preceding one. The two outer sections balance the middle. At m. 31, a quarter of the way through the work, is the *scherzando* flute melody. Slightly more than halfway through, at m. 60, the music starts a long buildup to the main climax of the movement which is at m. 88.

Slightly more than three quarters of the way through is the return of the opening at m. 91. This symmetry of proportion is a compositional technique of Ben-Haim's which is seen again and again in his works. The various sections are determined by their distinctive character, especially in relation to rhythm and melody.

Integrity

This movement is unified by the balance and contrast between the *recitativo* and the *scherzando* ideas.

This dichotomy produces a cohesive design which is coordinated through elements of contrast and repetition. Unity is also achieved through contrasting motivic ideas; for example the long-lined improvisatory opening in the viola and flute parts which contrasts strongly with the lighthearted, dance-like *scherzando* melody.

The climax is marked not only by *fortissimo* markings, but by the densest texture in the movement. After this point, the intensity and the volume dwindle down to the tranquility of the opening section.

Complexity

The composer begins with a dialogue between the two opening themes, first stated by the viola and then by the flute. This is repeated and is then followed by a statement from the cello at m. 18.

A new theme is introduced in the *Allegretto* section at m. 31 by the flute. Three main ideas dominate this movement: the recitativo opening and the jocular flute melody, marked *scherzando*. Variety is achieved by strong contrasts in tempo, dynamics and mood.

There is an interesting use of a pedal point consisting of a long trill in the cello at mm. 4, 12 and 83. The only time there is a pedal with no trill is in the *Allegretto* section and this consists of the note B repeated in higher and lower octaves.

As is often found in Ben-Haim's music, commas (mm. 8, 17) indicate a vocal conception.

Subtlety

The use of *con sordino* and *senza sordino* as well as glissandi and harmonics point to the various ways Ben-Haim creates special effects in this movement. Another example is the direction *senza vibrato* in the violin part, producing a less warm sound.

This movement has an unusual number of detailed instructions to the performers indicating subtle changes of tempo, timbre and dynamics.

Third Movement

Stylistic Level

Sonority

The dynamics of this movement range in intensity from *fff* at m. 126 to *pppp* in the very last measure. Although this work has a subdued sonority for the most part, there are occasional loud passages and strongly accented chords, often followed by *piano*.

There are three climaxes in this movement, the most dramatic one occurring at m. 106 and ending *fff* at mm. 126-127. This is immediately followed by a measure of rest with a fermata and a return to *pianissimo*. Words the composer uses, including *leggiero*, *pizzicato* and *grazzioso*, clearly call for a sprightly mood, which is achieved through non-legato execution. Although Ben-Haim brings the opening theme back an octave higher in the flute part at m. 129, this time it is marked *lento* and represents a dramatic tempo change from what came before.

The main climax of the work which begins at m. 106 and culminates at m. 127 has the highest registration and also some special effects such as long trills on very high notes in the flute part.

Harmony

There is no tonal center in much of this movement. The violin part begins using the C natural minor scale, but the cello part provides a bass which fails to provide a definite key center. The last chord of the movement is also ambiguous, containing an open fifth, C-G, but also containing a D. The use of the primitive open fifths used so often in other of Ben-Haim's works is found in the opening cello part and continues until m. 25. They occur again at m. 90 in the viola part.

Rhythm

Although the outer sections are in unchanged quadruple meter, the second section starting at m. 57 has a great many meter changes. This is especially true in the *presto* section, which rapidly shifts back and forth from duple to triple.

There are also tempo changes at important places in the movement. It begins *Andantino commodo e cantabile*; at m. 39, there is an *accelerando* and at m. 41 a new metronome marking (quarter equals 104). At m. 57 the original *Andantino* tempo is reestablished through the use of *L'istesso tempo*. At m. 86 a sudden change to *presto* begins the third section, which continues until m. 129 where the original material returns, highly embellished, in a *Lento* tempo.

Unlike the first and second movements, there is no metronome marking at the beginning of this one. Whether this is an oversight or intentional is impossible to determine.

Melody

The opening melody in the violin is organized into regular four-bar phrases and utilizes a neo-modal lyricism. It is then restated an octave higher in the flute and then starting at m. 42 is repeated in a new scale (E natural minor). A new theme is introduced by the flute at m. 57, which is characterized by much longer notes at the start, but then is extended with sextuplet and triplet sixteenth-note figures. The highest registration in the movement coincides with the biggest climax, at mm. 126-127.

When the opening melody returns at m. 129 it is in a much slower tempo (*lento*), and is greatly embellished.

Structural Level

Clarity

This movement consists of three distinct themes which are clearly set forth by tempo changes. The first theme begins the movement and is played by the violin. It is heard again at m. 34 in the flute part. The tempo increases due to an *accelerando* and at m. 42 a fragment of the first theme is heard again.

A new theme makes its appearance at m. 57, marked *L'istesso tempo*, also played by the flute. A third theme, resembling a tarantella, is heard at m. 86 and is marked *Presto*. Finally, the first theme returns in varied form at m. 129 at a *lento* tempo.

Proportion

This 149 measure movement is divided into four sections. A quarter of the way through, at m. 37, a crescendo begins which leads to the first significant climax. Slightly more than halfway through at m. 76 the next climax begins. Three quarters of the way through, m. 110 is the beginning of the main climax.

The two outer movements have an almost identical number of measures while the middle movement is the shorter of the three with 112 measures.

Integrity

Motivically, this movement is balanced by the long lyrical melody which introduces it and the contrasting triplet motif of the *Presto*. Although the second theme at m. 57 is broader, containing longer note values, it is expanded upon by sextuplet and triplet 16ths.

There is a similarity in conception between this movement and the second in that both have distinct sections delineated by strong tempo changes.

Complexity

Rhythmically, Ben-Haim provides a striking contrast by the way he shifts from slow cantabile sections to *Presto* scherzo-like passages. There are also contrasts in the way he uses Middle-Eastern melodies and synthesizes them with neo-modal harmonies, interspersed with contemporary dissonances.

Further contrast is provided by the juxtaposition of the long-lined flute melody against the triplet motif in the *Presto* section (m. 113).

Subtlety

Subtle gestures such as the *piano-sforzando* repetitions at m. 33 help to build excitement and intensity in the movement. Another touch is the dropping out of the flute from mm. 86 through 93, unusual, since this instrument has dominated the work up to this point. Another subtle detail is the use of an exclamation point after the word *piano* at m. 30.

After the loudest climax in the movement there is a measure of silence, prolonged by a fermata. This serves to introduce the last section, marked *Lento* where the flute returns with the opening melody and the strings accompany with mutes.

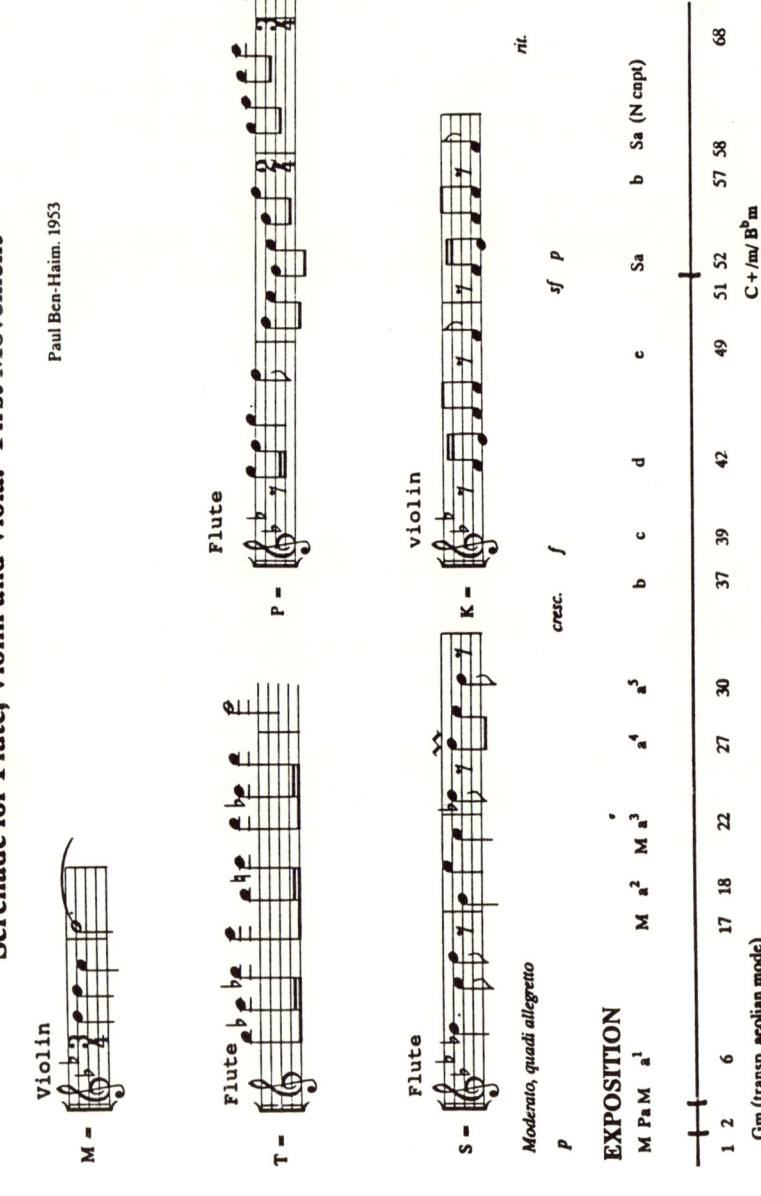

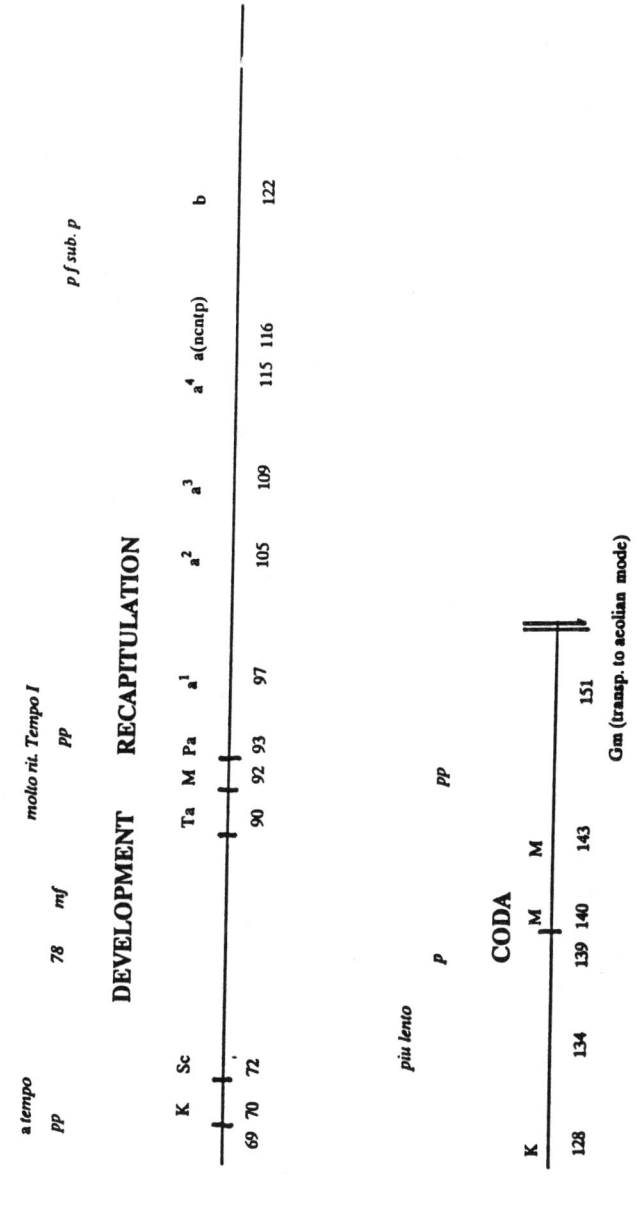

Serenade, Second Movement

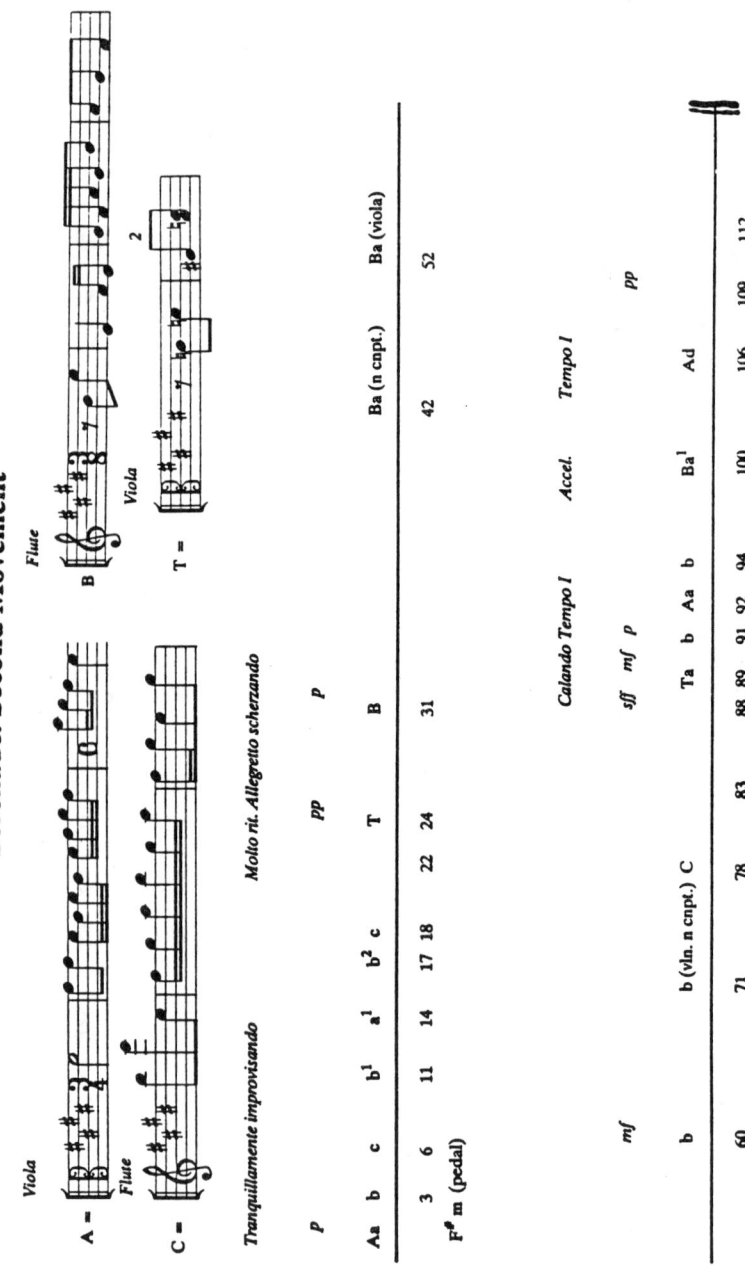

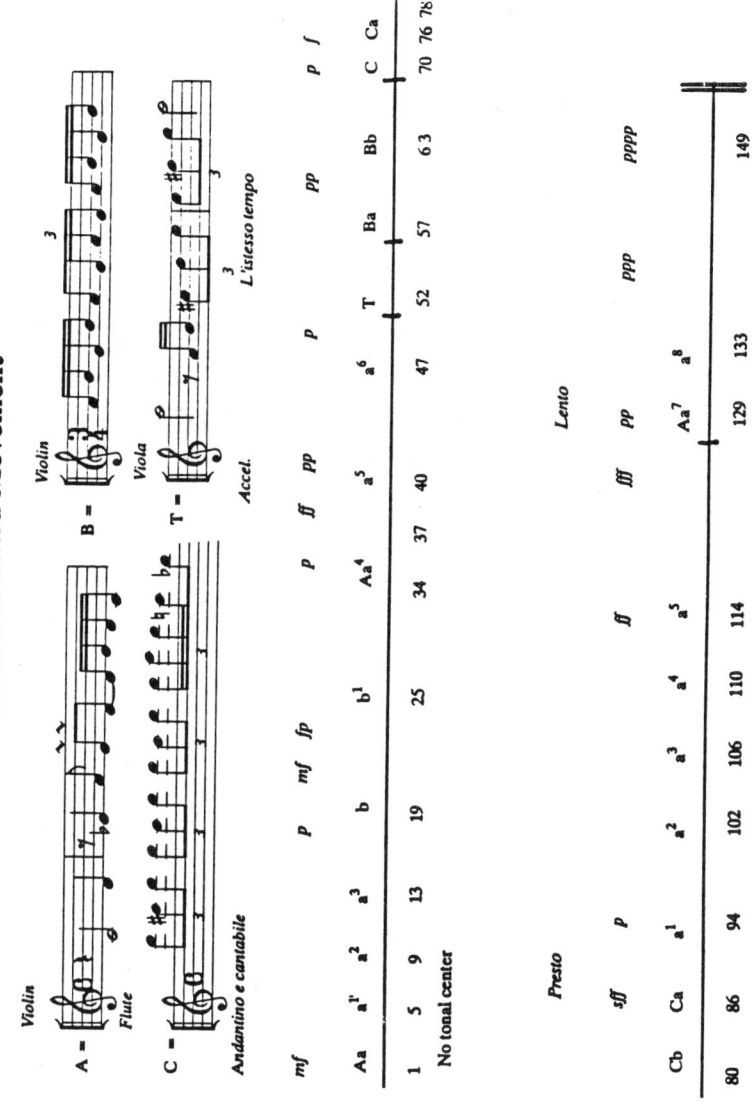

Serenade, Third Movement

Chapter Ten

IMPROVISATION AND DANCE FOR VIOLIN AND PIANO

1971

The *Improvisation and Dance* follows Ben-Haim's habit of assigning the pastoral and dance style for his chamber works as opposed to the Romantic tradition of his larger pieces. The style of the improvisation represents the character of Ben-Haim's trademark, pastorale, while the second *Theme* is literally the dance section, which is a contrasting form.

Stylistic Level

Sonority

Although there is a climax at m. 14 in the violin solo part which opens this work, the first climactic point occuring in both instruments is at mm. 100-110. This passage ends with a triple *sforzando* and is in fact the way the whole piece ends.

The range of sonority in this piece is from *pppp* to *fff*. The first triple *piano* occurs in the solo violin part at m. 4, very close to the beginning and the piece ends with a triple *sforzando*.

This work has its densest writing in the climactic sections, mm. 100-110, and mm. 251 to the end. However, instances occur where there is a propulsive forward motion such as the broken chord figures in the style of J. S. Bach, beginning at m. 200. These also lead to strong climaxes even though the texture is thin.

As is Ben-Haim's habit, climactic points also correspond to the highest register in both instruments, as at m. 105. This piece has markings as diverse as *cantando, con sordino, lontano* and as well as *senza sordino, marcato, and martellato.*

Harmony

The Aeolian mode figures prominently throughout this piece. However, it is difficult to pinpoint a definite tonal center, and of course as in most of his works, Ben-Haim provides no key signature. There are strong elements of bi-tonality as in the measure where the piano enters. The solo violin has an E to A glissando while underneath this, the piano has a slow arpeggio starting with F-sharp and B-flat. The "Dance Theme" starting at m. 57 is in the minor dominant. There is a playful, almost teasing use of the harmony in this passage which keeps going from B-flat in the trill to B-natural.

This piece is balanced by a contrapuntal style of writing beginning at m. 23, which continues in the same style until the "Dance Theme" is reached (m. 57). This section is largely homophonic. There is a brief role-reversal at m. 156 where the violin plays the accompaniment and the piano has the melody.

Rhythm

There is much complex rhythmic activity in the work and also many changes of tempo. The first direction, *molto rubato* shows the improvisatory nature of this piece and demands a free, flexible and imaginative interpretation. A new section is always indicated by a new tempo marking. There are also many changes in meter in the opening improvisation section, but when the dance section begins, the meter is mainly duple and changes very little. In sum, where Ben-Haim wants an expressive, improvisatory quality the music is mainly triple meter; where he wants a driving, perpetual-motion effect, the meter is duple.

Because of the varied rhythms which open the work and are found throughout, and the driving, toccata-like quality to some of the piano accompaniment, this piece lives up to its title.

Melody

This piece is comprised of two very clear and contrasting themes. The first is the rather meditative, dotted motif which is found throughout the opening section, while the second, at m. 57, has a driving vitality which contrasts with the cantabile opening.

The first theme is disjunct, while the second is much closer intervalically.

The shifting meter and the contrasting themes are balanced by a modal harmonic structure. Most of the transitions are accomplished by using motivic fragments to produce a seamless bridge from one part to another.

Structural Level

Clarity

The seven sections of this work are clearly set apart by changes of tempo. The first section, *molto rubato* ends at m. 23. The next, *Andantino lusingando,* continues through m. 42. *Piu tranquillo (come prima)* harks back to the opening measures. The fourth section, *Allegro grazioso* continues through m. 130, where a new section marked *Largamente, con languidezza* continues through m. 156. *Presto* marks the beginning of the sixth section and this continues until the closing material, marked *Meno mosso* at m. 241.

As is Ben-Haim's habit, climactic points also correspond to the highest register in both instruments, as at m. 105. This piece has markings as diverse as *cantando, con sordino, lontano* and as well as *senza sordino, marcato, and martellato*.

Harmony

The Aeolian mode figures prominently throughout this piece. However, it is difficult to pinpoint a definite tonal center, and of course as in most of his works, Ben-Haim provides no key signature. There are strong elements of bi-tonality as in the measure where the piano enters. The solo violin has an E to A glissando while underneath this, the piano has a slow arpeggio starting with F-sharp and B-flat. The "Dance Theme" starting at m. 57 is in the minor dominant. There is a playful, almost teasing use of the harmony in this passage which keeps going from B-flat in the trill to B-natural.

This piece is balanced by a contrapuntal style of writing beginning at m. 23, which continues in the same style until the "Dance Theme" is reached (m. 57). This section is largely homophonic. There is a brief role-reversal at m. 156 where the violin plays the accompaniment and the piano has the melody.

Rhythm

There is much complex rhythmic activity in the work and also many changes of tempo. The first direction, *molto rubato* shows the improvisatory nature of this piece and demands a free, flexible and imaginative interpretation. A new section is always indicated by a new tempo marking. There are also many changes in meter in the opening improvisation section, but when the dance section begins, the meter is mainly duple and changes very little. In sum, where Ben-Haim wants an expressive, improvisatory quality the music is mainly triple meter; where he wants a driving, perpetual-motion effect, the meter is duple.

Because of the varied rhythms which open the work and are found throughout, and the driving, toccata-like quality to some of the piano accompaniment, this piece lives up to its title.

Melody

This piece is comprised of two very clear and contrasting themes. The first is the rather meditative, dotted motif which is found throughout the opening section, while the second, at m. 57, has a driving vitality which contrasts with the cantabile opening.

The first theme is disjunct, while the second is much closer intervalically.

The shifting meter and the contrasting themes are balanced by a modal harmonic structure. Most of the transitions are accomplished by using motivic fragments to produce a seamless bridge from one part to another.

Structural Level

Clarity

The seven sections of this work are clearly set apart by changes of tempo. The first section, *molto rubato* ends at m. 23. The next, *Andantino lusingando,* continues through m. 42. *Piu tranquillo (come prima)* harks back to the opening measures. The fourth section, *Allegro grazioso* continues through m. 130, where a new section marked *Largamente, con languidezza* continues through m. 156. *Presto* marks the beginning of the sixth section and this continues until the closing material, marked *Meno mosso* at m. 241.

Proportion

There are 258 measures in this work. The significant sections are stated at strategic points in this piece. An example of this is the dance theme which comes a little earlier than a quarter of the way through at m. 57. Exactly half way through at m. 130 there is an important variant of the dance theme and the marking *Largamente, con languidezza*, indicating a change of character as well as tempo. A little more than three quarters of the way through, the Bach-like figurations, marked *leggiermente saltando* begin. This continues until nearly the end of the piece.

The dance theme dominates the piece, with the improvisation theme functioning like an introduction and then at the end as a coda. This plan provides a solid architectural basis for the music.

Integrity

This piece is constructed with two contrasting themes. The first is rather disjunct and dreamy, in an improvisatory style. The second theme, introduced at m. 57 with a short piano introduction, is more straightforward, dance-like and staccato in character. These two themes are in striking contrast to one another. There is also a bit of material, introduced in the violin at m. 16 which is more like a recitative than what follows it.

Complexity

The two places where the writing is most uncomplicated is where Ben-Haim introduces the two main themes. The first theme is introduced by the solo violin part which extends for 15 measures without the piano accompaniment. The second theme is introduced by a simple rhythmic and harmonic idea. Much of the rest of the work, in contrast, is denser in texture, especially the last page which runs the gamut of dynamic levels from *pianissimo* to triple *sforzando*.

Subdued and meditative passages are balanced by energetic, fiery perpetual motion sections, until in an explosion of sound the composer makes his powerful final statement.

Subtlety

An interesting detail of this work is the opening, which consists of 15 measures of solo violin. This device is in keeping with the improvisatory nature of the piece. There is a jarring dissonance at the piano's entrance where the violin's E to A slide clashes with the F-sharp and B-flat in the accompaniment.

Great contrast is provided by the section marked *Allegro grazioso* where the music is much simpler and more straightforward.

The composer uses many violinistic devices such as *Con sordino* at the opening, *spiccato* bowing (m.31), harmonics (m. 49), *glissando* (m. 110) and *saltando* bowing (m. 201), which is a bouncing bow effect.

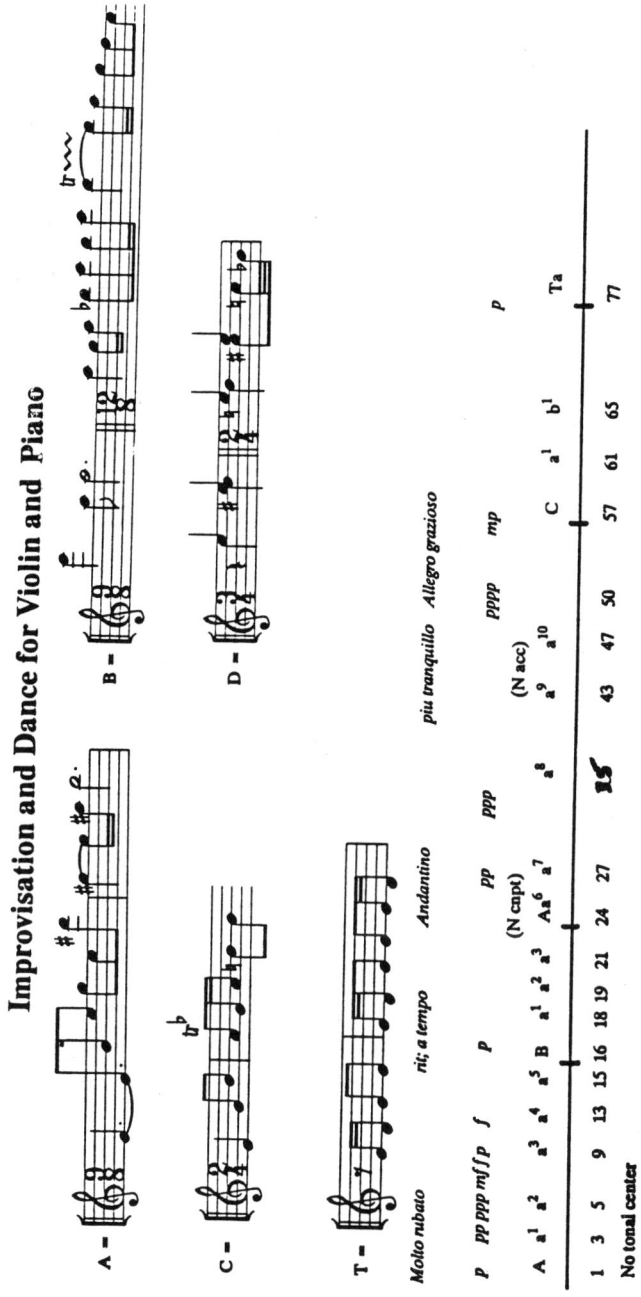

Improvisation and Dance (continued)

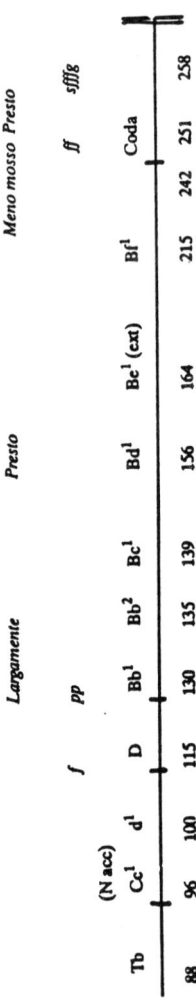

Chapter Eleven

ARABIC SONG
For Solo Voice Or Instrument And Piano Accompaniment

1962

This piece can be compared to an "arabesque" (an Arab derived word). The *Webster's 7th Collegiate Dictionary* defines "arabesque" as "an ornament or style which produces an intricate pattern of interlaced, sometimes angular and sometimes curved lines."

Though simple, the melody also contains an ornamental interweaving of detail corresponding to the definition of an arabesque.

Stylistic Level

Sonority

Although the accompaniment is largely in the background, the solo part (voice or instrument) is quite impassioned. It starts out *mezzo forte* and proceeds in an improvisatory manner with frequent meter changes and changes of tempo. As the piece unfolds the melody rises to forte at m. 10. and reaches the main climax at m. 18. At m. 23 the dynamic level falls and the music returns to *piano* and then to *pianissimo* at m. 26. The accompaniment ends the piece with *ppp*.

The range of the melody is largely in the middle register; however, Ben-Haim creates excitement by other means, mainly by using irregular meters and interesting rhythmical patterns such as sextuplets (m.10) and eighth-quarter triplets (m. 13). Also, the fluctuation between the original *andantino* tempo and the rubato areas create a sense of tension and spontaneity.

The mood created in this work is one of mystery and passion, reflecting the Westerner's view of the Arabic world.

Harmony

Ben-Haim provides the key signature for E minor but that tonality is not clearly established in this piece. As is his style, he avoids any strong feeling of key center and ends the work with a stress on the dominant, B. This pitch is present, if not emphasized, in nearly every measure. The tone D-sharp, is also prominent and one finds it functioning as the leading-tone (ti-do). It is also used with C-natural (lay-ti) as the augmented second in the harmonic minor scale, a characteristic sound in Middle Eastern music.

Rhythm

This piece is mostly in duple meter except for one instance of 3/4 time in m. 9, and three instances of 5/4 time at mm. 20, 21 and 23. This unusual meter often serves to extend the melodic material. Following the truly improvisatory character of this piece, there are many tempo changes, beginning with the solo's entrance in m. 2. There follow many *accelerando* markings, as well as *a tempo* and *rubato*.

Melody

There are two melodic ideas dominating the piece. The first opens the work and exploits the augmented second, C-natural, D-sharp. The second one, more clearly in E major, begins at m.

13 and emphasizes the dominant note, B. The range of the solo part is uncharacteristically narrow so as to accommodate the voice. There is a variant of the second idea in simpler form at m. 18. The opening melody returns almost unchanged at the end of the piece, but the accompaniment is quite different, marked *secco* and *staccato*, in contrast to the mysterious quality of the beginning.

In the piano accompaniment the note B serves as a pedal point and opens and closes the work. This note is also echoed many times in the solo part.

Structural Level

Clarity

The design of the work is ternary. The opening idea in the solo part extends from mm. 2 through 8. The material from mm. 10 through 12 can be considered a transition. The theme of the middle section starts at m. 13 and suggests the key of E major. This theme is varied (simplified) at m. 18 and is followed by three measures of transitional material. The opening theme returns at m. 24 with very few changes from the original. Its reappearance is heralded by a return to *Tempo primo*

Proportion

The first 12 measures comprise the opening theme and the transition. The next 12 measures include the second theme and its variant. The return of the opening is incorporated in the last 8 measures, which overlap the previous material. Significant sections are introduced in architecturally important places.

The main climax of the work comes slightly after the middle, at m. 18 and is preceded by an *accelerando*.

Integrity

This piece is unified through the opening melody which returns nearly intact at m. 23. The piano accompaniment is very different; only at m. 26 and in the penultimate measure is there a reference to the broken octaves of the opening.

The transition, beginning at m. 8 is heralded by an *accelerando* which establishes a new tempo for the second theme.

Motivically, the piece is unified by augmented seconds in the opening and closing sections and by the 8th and two 16ths pattern, found in nearly every measure.

Complexity

In its 30 measures, this piece exhibits a remarkable variety of moods and great ingenuity in creating them. The first theme, whose range is only a minor 7th, is haunting and evocative of the composer's Middle Eastern milieu. The accompaniment is harmonically ambiguous and impressionistic. On its return at m. 23, there are tiny variants; for example the grace-note B in m. 4 is omitted in the corresponding place in m. 25. The two 8ths following the grace-note in m. 4 become a 16th and a dotted 8th in m. 25. This change also in volves the two 8ths on the second beat in m. 7; in m. 28 they also become an 16th and a dotted 8th.

The accompaniment at the return of the opening melody is a complete contrast from the beginning. It is dry and rhythmical, evocative of small drums, bells and cymbals.

Subtlety

A close study of the similarities and differences between the two themes and their return reveal several subtle changes. For example, at m. 16 there are grace-notes preceeding the E's; at the parallel passage in m. 22, they are replaced by 16th-notes. The B's in m. 13 are embellished by C-sharps; in the parallel place at m. 18 they stand unadorned. The two triplets on the third and fourth beats are changed to plain 8th-notes in m. 18.

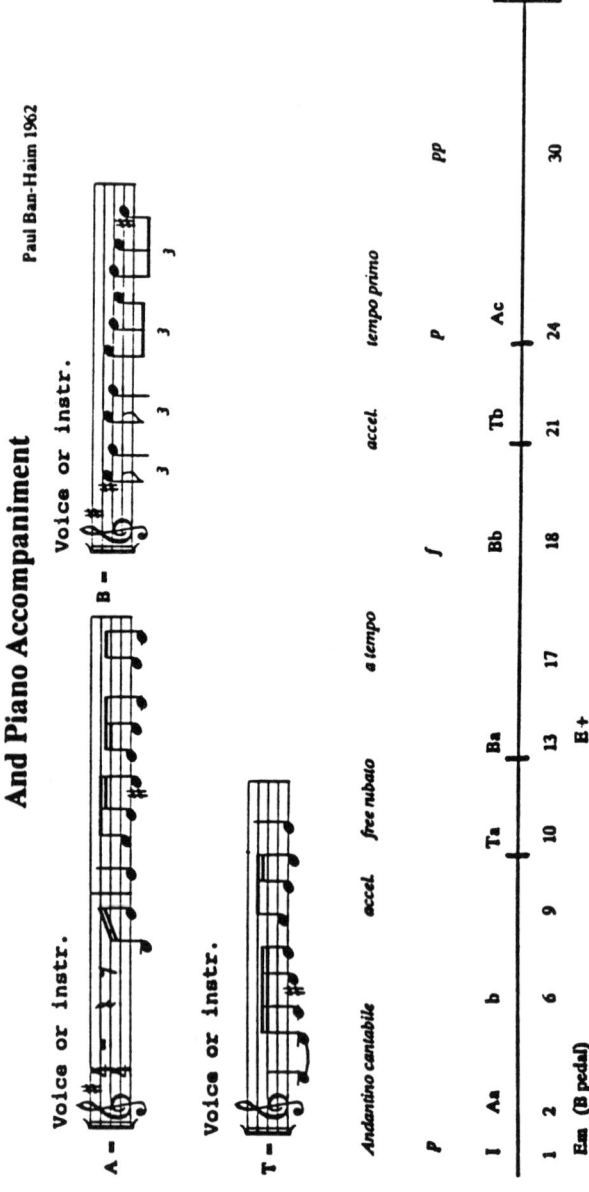

Chapter Twelve

PERFORMANCE GUIDE

SONATINA OP. 38

The Sonatina, Op. 38 is one of Ben-Haim's finest works for solo piano, both in its form and gentle lyricism. Though the composer creates a tightly woven work structurally, to this listener, there is more quality music here than in some larger-scale works by better known composers.

Paul Ben-Haim's Sonatina for piano solo is an excellent example of his pastoral style, and is also representative of his Oriental-sounding melodies and Western harmonies.

First Movement

The piece opens with a graceful, lilting melody and should be played with a light touch and a dancing quality on the surface of the keys. However, any tendency to rush should be avoided. As pointed out in the La Rue analysis, the overall sonority is subdued. The left hand must be very legato, while the right hand is staccato.

At m. 5, although the left hand gets busier with its 16th notes, the right hand should be given more emphasis and the whole notes in the bass of mm. 6-7 should sound through. Because so much of Ben-Haim's music is composed of melodic fragments, the performer should think in long phrases.

The first musical paragraph ends at m. 12 and a long crescendo must be made until the *forte* of m. 12.

When the opening theme is repeated at m. 13 a different color is called for, with a little heavier sound than at the opening. All trills and long notes may be pedaled.

At m. 17, a more agitated section begins. Pedal should be used at the beginning of each sixteenth-note group and the hand should shape each phrase using a flexible wrist which turns in the direction of the music. M. 21 is the second theme, a rhythmic variation of the opening motif. It needs to "breathe" as indicated by the comma at m. 22. The top notes of chords, such as the one in the right hand of m. 25, must sing out over the running bass. This is a problem of balance, since there is much less tone in the short strings of the upper register than in the long, heavy bass strings. Leaning toward the right-hand fifth finger will be helpful.

The next section beginning at m. 36 and continuing to 46 needs to sound impressionistic and must sound as though coming out of a fog. A quarter pedal can be used to achieve this effect. Bring out the left hand at m. 41 at m. 43, the walking fifths in the bass require an in-and-out motion, especially where there are black notes. From m. 47 on to the climax at m. 53, more arm weight and a loose wrist are necessary to produce a bigger sound. The weight and power should be transmitted to the keyboard from the shoulder.

The Recapitulation section starting at m. 54 requires a very light touch to produce a muffled tone quality. A quarter pedal may be used until the more open style of writing builds to a crescendo at m. 66. The performer should drop on the chords at m. 67 so as to avoid a harsh, percussive sound. The quintuplets and sextuplets (m. 64-66) carefully paced so as not to sound rushed.

Second Movement

As the analysis shows, the touch stone of interpretation for this movement is Ben-Haim's direction, *Improvvisazione*. It must always be kept in mind that one must strive for a certain spontaneity and simplicity of sound. To create that effect, the tempo should be correct but not unyielding, and with a generous use of rubato; on the first page alone, there are seven meter changes. The music must breathe as if being sung, and care should be taken to observe the commas which the composer adds for this purpose. The dynamic level is subdued and this must always be kept in mind as a key to the overall rendition.

There is a general rule of interpretation which says that when short notes follow a long note, the short ones must be played at a softer dynamic level. In other words, since the volume of the note decays on the piano, one must used the sound that is "left over" for the remaining notes. This rule applies to the opening measure of this movement and all similar situations.

For a beautiful tone, one must drop into the first note of m. 1, using the fleshy part of the fingertip. The thirty-second-note embellishment in m. 2 should evolve out of the preceding B flats and be played like a cadenza. In m. 8, the chords in the left hand are rolled slowly with pedal. Although ornaments in slow movements are generally played slowly, there are times when the opposite is called for, and one such instance is at m. 10 where the embellishment should be light and fast.

In the next section marked *calmo*, there is a curious anomaly in that the metronome setting calls for a quicker rate of speed than in the opening *Andantino*. Therefore, the performer must not drag the beat, even though the tempo marking indicates it.

The bass-line at m. 14 must sing with a full expansive sound, much like a cello. At 16, the entrance of an alto voice should point up the imitative counter point and at 18, the quarters in the soprano should stand out above the faster moving lower parts.

At m. 24, the trills are difficult because the player must release the notes of the rolled chord under the trill and then end slightly early in order to play the next chord with security. Further on, as the texture thickens, the performer is still required to maintain a low dynamic level and the temptation to rush should be avoided.

At Tempo I (m. 33) is the first forte marking in the movement and this only holds for the next few measures. At m. 40 the grace notes are light, slow and before the beat. A careful examination of the pedal marking for the last four measures of the movement shows that the composer wants the minor thirds to sound alone, without the background of bass sounds.

Third Movement

This movement is an example of Lisztian style; a "perpetual motion" machine with its virtuostic writing, resembling a toccata, requiring rhythmic energy, an inner intensity and a sense of direction. It should be noted that unless otherwise indicated, the sixteenth notes are to be played legato and the eighths staccato, sharp, short and close to the keys. It is advisable to practice this movement slowly and make sure that every note is securely under the fingers before attempting a faster speed.

Ben-Haim's metronome marking of 176 to a quarter is somewhat unrealistic, especially in places where there are skips, such as m. 23 for example. It should also be noted that the coda is marked *Presto* which calls for an even faster tempo. The movement should be played as fast as the performer can go while still maintaining control. Steady, articulate passage work will always sound faster than a mere scramble to get the notes in.

The left hand open fifths should be phrased as follows:

Example 32. *Sonatina*, 3rd Movement, m 1.

which is a much more interesting way to treat the bass.

The player must remember that the prevailing dynamic is piano until m. 19, and should consequently hold back the sound, although all accents and climaxes are important. At mm. 9, 10 and 11, note that the *fortes* are followed by *pianos*.

The rhythmic design at m. 13 is reminiscent of the Israeli national dance, the *Hora*, with its rest-chord- rest-chord, suggesting a hopping dance step.

At m. 32 Ben-Haim's pedal mark should be followed fearlessly, even though there are scale-wise passages in the deep bass; this cascade of sound is the specific effect he wanted. The sixteenths may be played with the right hand, while the left may play the low D-flats, if necessary.

At the *Presto* all caution can at last be thrown to the winds. Beginning triple *piano*, the blind octaves should build to the performer's loudest and fastest playing.

Five Pieces for Piano

Pastorale

As the analysis shows, this first piece creates an impressionistic sound with the use of the pentatonic scale, immediately calling to mind music of East and West. The *Harvard Dictionary of Music* defines "Pastorale":

> Instrumental or vocal pieces written in imitation of the music of shepherds, their shawms and pipes... in moderate time, suggestive of a lullaby, tender flowing melody, and long held drones.

This describes Ben-Haim's piece perfectly. *Moderatamente mosso e quasi improvisando* in the opening directions implies a certain freedom necessary for the proper interpretation of this piece.

The opening four 32nd notes going to the quarter need to be shaped with a high wrist, as do all similar measures. The first four measures are split into a phrasing scheme of two-plus-two, but mm. 1 and 2 should be given more weight than the ones which follow. Mm. 5-8 are an elaboration of the beginning and require a more open sound with a *crescendo,* while m. 7, marked *pianissimo* and *lontano* (distant), may be split between the two hands, the first A being taken with the left hand. It should be mentioned that in much of this piece, the melody's goal is always a half-note or quarter-note, either of which should be emphasized.

Mm. 3 through 16 are an elaborated extension of the first two measures. The left hand represents a bagpipe drone to which notes are added, creating a cluster of chords; the thicker the chords, the more arm-weight must be used. The grace notes at calando (m. 16) should not be too fast, in keeping with the character of a pastorale.

At m. 17 as the initial ideas are further developed, particular attention should be paid to details such as accents and staccato dots. A delicate sound should continue, but should be "marked yet simple," as indicated in Italian. The best way to be simple is to be decisive about what to bring out.

Long phrases such as mm. 19-20 are to be thought of in small groups, and it should be kept in mind that the texture is polyphonic.

At m. 30, where the opening material is recapitulated, a distant, yet sonorous sound is called for; the word *Sognoso* is used, which means "dreamy." The last chord should be held until it fades into nothingness.

Intermezzo

This piece has a whimsical quality with its syncopated anacrusis and thin texture, in keeping with its title, which means, "a theatrical entertainment of light character . . . between more serious works." The unusual Italian direction *trasognato* means, "lost in a reverie."

In mm. 1-3 the double stemmed dotted quarters have broken slurs, indicating a *portato* touch; not quite connecting one dotted quarter to the next, producing a bell-like effect. These measures build to the E-flat dotted half note in m. 4. The *rubato* in m. 4 should be light yet with an improvisatory quality. This piece consists of two unrelated ideas: the motif in m. 1 and the 16th notes marked *rubato.* in m. 4, which are both expanded upon and developed.

At m. 11, although the melody is reinforced with Ben-Haim's characteristic double fourths, this passage calls for a flexible wrist and a graceful sound. The long notes may be played with quarter pedal and polyrythms, which occur frequently, should be practiced with the metronome for greater security. The analysis shows that these polyrhythms as well as the use of syncopation enhance the rhythmic scheme.

At m. 21, although the right hand is very busy with 16th notes, it is the left hand which must be heard and this part continues to predominate in the ensuing measures. A crescendo is called for from mm. 24 through 29, but becomes no louder than *mezzo forte.*

At m. 32 the opening motif is recalled and should be played pianissimo, like a distant memory. The rhythm here somewhat resembles a *siciliano*, which is defined in the *Harvard Dictionary* as follows:

> A 17th and 18th century dance type of Sicilian origin, in very moderate 6/8 or 12/8 meter, usually with a flowing broken-chord accompaniment and a soft, lyrical melody with dotted rhythms — similar if not identical in character to the pastorale.

The long notes in the last four measures should be held for their full value, and the last two notes in the extreme bass may be played slightly apart because there are five *p's* marked there.

Capriccio Agitato

Although the title of this piece contains two words, the interpretation should be influenced more by *agitato* than *capriccio.* The analysis points out that most of this piece is marked *forte* or *fortissimo* with only a few *pianos* or *pianissimos* interspersed. Also, scales undulating in a wave-like manner create sonorous wash of sound.

The opening 32nd-note runs should be played brilliantly in an unbroken line, creating a dramatic and stormy effect. The distribution of the notes between the two hands may be altered according to the player's preference.

The pianist must possess a solid technique to perform this piece well. The notes must be articulated and the destination of every small phrase must be shown. The chords at m. 5 need solid arm-weight and a separate attack on each one, even though the first three after the rest are an anacrusis.

The performer should make sure that the soprano part (m. 16, etc.) sings out above the torrents of sound underneath. To this end, it is essential to play the 16th-note sextuplets as softly as possible.

Canzonetta

Ben-Haim's conception of this piece is indeed a "lyrical song," coming in between the two fiery outer movements. In addition, the expressive indication at the beginning is *affettuoso*, meaning "affectionate, with warmth."

The opening section resembles a nocturne with its melancholy, reflective mood in the right-hand melody and widely spaced, arpeggiated bass. Although the right hand plays chords, it is always the top notes that must sing out, as indicated by the *tenuto* marks above the chords. To aid in achieving this effect, the right hand must lean toward the fifth finger. Such voicing will produce the *cantando* quality required by Ben-Haim.

The next, though thematically related section starts at m. 17 marked *amoroso*, like a memory of what came before, the pianist must literally "caress" the keys. Because the texture is thinner and the dynamic marking is *pianissimo*, the performer should aim for a gentler sound. This movement alternates between improvisatory and impressionistic waves of sound and sharp marcato passages.

Note that unlike the beginning, a *tenuto* mark is only placed on the first beat of each measure, and commas are used to show places where the music must "breathe" in the style of a singer.

Toccata

When executed properly, this piece can be very exciting; the main point to remember is not to give away too much too soon; the player must bring the audience to the music.

The performer needs to observe the *presto* indication as closely as possible, bringing out a note where appropriate, or making accents at the beginning of phrases. In general this work of bravura virtuosity needs tremendous rhythmic energy and a sense direction, as mentioned in the analysis.

A logical fingering for the first few measures is to use the third finger in both the right and left hands on the E and to take the D in m. 2 with the left hand thumb. The phrasing should be conceived of as always starting from the second note, leading to the first note of the next measure. Where certain phrases repeat (mm. 17-20 and 21-24), the second phrase should be like an echo. At m. 26 the sound may be a little more open for a short period, to highlight the introduction of double notes, making sure to follow Ben- Haim's dynamic markings. Any *sforzandi* such as the one at m. 37 need a high and flexible wrist. It is helpful to remember that the wrists are "shock absorbers" as Josef Lhevinne called them.[1]

Since this work is another example of perpetual motion, breathing spaces should be premeditated, as in m. 37, after the eighth note (see analysis). In the opening pages, "Toccata" is a piece which builds momentum like a speeding train, and sometimes more energy than sound is called for.

Note in mm. 47-49 that each third on the first beat has an incomplete slur. This implies a touch of pedal and the illusion of connecting one third to the next, although actually binding them together would be inappropriate. At mm. 51-57, a practical fingering is essential and should be written in by the performer, conforming to the individual shape of his hand. Also, the analysis states that the introduction of the 8th rest on the first beat, gives added rhythmical excitement.

Mm. 55-57 may be played *mezzo forte* with an accent on the right hand's D in m. 53 which is the high point of the passage. The same accent should be placed at the same relative point in the following phrase. It is important to keep the left hand very staccato, while the right hand plays legato at mm. 51-57. It would be helpful to stay close to the keys in order to produce a sharp staccato.

At m. 70 a quarter pedal may be used, but the performer should get no louder than piano as the octaves in the bass will sound anyway. The pedal point B in the right hand should be held down lightly so as not to produce stiffness. The left-hand melody starting at m. 70 is a restatement and expansion of the opening motif. Only the first pair of octaves at m. 70 needs an accent, and any notes which change in the bass need to be brought out.

The first important climax is at m. 94, which should be built up to with a crescendo from m. 90. However, a quick diminuendo is necessary to reestablish Ben-Haim's piano in m. 96. The half-note E natural at mm. 101 and 104 needs more arm-weight because the texture starting at m. 97 is thicker, and this note must sound through each time.

M. 116 introduces a more melodic section which recalls a Middle Eastern, melismatic, quarter-tone chant. The analysis also shows that m. 119 is the only instance where there is truly contrasting material and should be brought out. From m. 121 in particular clear articulation is needed as well as a good fingering. Again the left hand is to be played staccato with accented notes especially at harmonic changes, while the right hand sings a legato line. The wrist may be lifted before dropping onto the trills at m. 134 and similar places.

Pedal should be used on the C octaves at m. 143 and chords of longer value. As the texture gets thicker, it would be advisable to utilize increasing weight from the shoulder as well as additional pedaling.

The music constantly builds to its final climax at m. 192, marked *con tutta forza*, which needs even more left hand and should be played with complete abandon. The finale is appropriately brilliant with its *martallato* marking and the blind octaves just before the end. (See analysis).

At m. 204, marked *diminuendo molto*, the dynamics may be at a lower level, but the inherent energy of the piece must never flag. There is a final powerful chord at m. 216, and then a downward slashing run followed by a pregnant pause.

Melody and Variations

1950

Unlike most sets of variations, which consist of a series of separate segments, these run into each other, often without any break in the music. It is probably for this reason that Ben-Haim did not use numbers at the beginning of each one. The whole piece is more integrated than are most examples of theme and variation, as mentioned in the analysis.

Ben-Haim's indication, *calmo e senza espressione* must be carefully followed in order to project the child-like simplicity and pastoral character of the theme. Its narrow range and repetitive motif creates an atmosphere of unpretentious tranquility. On the interpretation of the variations, Ben-Haim has written:

> I should like the pianist to bear the history of the little work well in mind when he performs it: it should be stated in a simple and innocent fashion and gradually develop in force and expressiveness; the resumption of the

theme at the conclusion of the work should be played very tenderly, without nuances or colouring just like the melody itself. I do not favour any rubato in the performance of this work, except where I have expressly demanded it.[2]

When performing this piece, the pianist would be wise to play the frequent repetitions (mm. 1-3, etc.) with varying dynamics. The first two notes, which are slurred, require a "down-up" motion. The E's on the third beat need an accent in both hands, and all notes with *tenuto* markings are to be brought out. At m. 5, where the melody is one step higher, more sound is necessary. All mordents are particularly important because they highlight the longer quarter notes and the analysis shows how they bring out a Middle-Eastern flavor.

Since the pedal markings are few and far between, they should be scrupulously observed. Note that many of them are at the end of the variation.

Allegretto

Since Ben-Haim did not number the variations, the author will use his Italian tempo indications as headings.

The first variation is marked *allegretto* and the meter signature is now cut time, indicating a quickening of the beat. The elaborated melody has a more dance-like quality so the performer should follow the rests carefully, as well as all phrasing indications. It is important to bring out the long notes in the bass (mm. 17-20) and to follow carefully all breathing pauses indicated by commas.

Un poco piu mosso

This variation, with its widely spaced, arpeggiated bass and lyrical melody is reminiscent of a nocturne and should be approached with tenderness and grace.

Note that on the third beats of all measures except the penultimate one, there are trills instead of mordents. These trills must note be cut short. In m. 36, the performer should bring out the change of mode in the bass, from major to minor.

Accelerando . . . vivo

The transition between the previous variation and this one is tricky as the player must follow Ben-Haim's pedal markings religiously. What he wishes is for the last interval of a second (G-A) to blend in with the low D (m. 49). The pedal is maintained through the first measure of the accelerando and the player has only two measures to reach the required *Vivo* tempo. This variation, in the style of a toccata, would benefit from a light but firm touch. However, as the intervals become larger, a more open sound is needed. Because the eighth-note motif begins with an anacrusis, all subsequent phrases must be thought of as starting on the second beat.

Molto calmo

Like a tune played on a shepherd's pipe, the five-four meter signature and the frequent use of thirty- second-note sextuplets give the music the character of an improvisation. Because of all these elements, rubato is appropriate. While the right hand busily weaves its melismatic, chant, the left hand must not be ignored.

The bell-like fourth in m. 85 is best played by crossing over with the left hand. This also will enable the performer to hold the tied note more easily.

Allegro giusto

This variation recalls a syncopated *hora* rhythm. The phrasing of the opening motif demands a "down-up" motion of the wrist, with more emphasis given to the accented half notes, as well as the rests. At m. 93 the staccato parallel fourths will be best executed by "throwing" the wrist. M. 97, with its thicker texture, calls for more arm-weight which will produce a fuller tone. The three eighth-note chords which appear on the second half of the third beats of mm. 97-99 lead to the open fifth in the bass on the first beat of the following measure.

Molto vivo

The performer must feel a strong pulse and a sense of forward propulsion in order to capture the energy inherent in this variation, as the analysis shows. Because of the fact that the first three measures are very similar, varying dynamics are essential. In this case it is suggested that the player make a *diminuendo* from *forte* to the *mezzo piano* in m. 107. In m. 108 the left hand must play with a sharply accented staccato.

Allegretto grazzioso

Ben-Haim's dotted lines show that he wants the player to think of the seven-four meter as consisting of three plus four groupings. However, the overall melodic line must be maintained.

The tricky left hand skips in m. 121 will be more secure if the performer plays the first chord and rests silently on the next. At m. 129 the melody is more legato as indicated by slurs in both hands as well as fewer rests in the right-hand part.

Lento e Rubato

Because of its long-lined improvisatory style, this variation is like a cantor's chant at a solemn, religious occasion. The tendency toward choppiness, caused by the extensive use of dotted rhythms, should inspire the performer to think in terms of long melodic lines. Ben-Haim's breathing comma at m. 141 shows them to be four-bar phrases.

At m. 144, it is helpful to think of the right hand as a flute part, while the left hand is like a plucked cello.

The performer should not forget to bring out the D pedal point at m. 148.

Allegro

The next variation, as is customary, follows the preceding one without a break. It begins in an impressionistic haze, mysterious and threatening, out of which sudden, drum-like motifs appear and disappear.

Beginning at m. 169 the pedal is not specifically marked, but its use is implied by Ben-Haim's broken slurs in the bass, making the accented seconds last somewhat longer than written. The absence of pedal is indicated by the word *secco*.

Piu mosso

In contrast to the previous variation, this one is dry and percussive. There is a similarity to the third movement of the composer's *Sonatina*, with its perpetual motion, and machine-like propulsion, as the analysis shows. It is necessary to articulate clearly because the left hand is sharply staccato while the right hand sings a legato line.

At m. 178, it will be helpful to think of the last D in the left hand as leading into the following interval of a second, so as to facilitate the leap.

The first notes in the left hand part which are clearly not played staccato begin on the third beat of m. 186 and should be held accordingly.

L'istesso tempo

The syncopated rhythm of this variation creates an atmosphere of seriousness and reflection. The left hand would benefit by dropping from a slight distance onto the first open fifth half-notes, and a "down-up" motion in the right hand on the opening slurred quarter going to the eighth. All the whole notes in the right hand should be held lightly so as not to stiffen the hand, as the player must execute the detached chords at the same time.

As there is a thickening of the texture throughout this piece, more weight is needed starting from mm. 198-199 and a crescendo is in order.

The octave passage at m. 205 requires a big, broad sound, but must not overpower the *fortissimo* climax at m. 209.

Molto vivo ed appassionato

As indicated by the *accelerando* in m. 209, the player has only one measure to establish the *molto vivo* tempo.

Again Ben-Haim's dashes in the 7/8 measures show that he means the player to think of the groupings as four plus three. The performer must remember to go down to the bottom of the key to produce the full sound required for much of this movement. Passages such as the octaves in mm. 215-216, which move forward in a long line, should be played in an improvisatory manner as demanded by the frequently shifting meter.

This variation, unlike the others, needs to be played with great abandon and a bigger tone. We now see infrequently used indications such as *espressivo molto* at m. 227.

Lento e pianissimo sin al fine

This final variation reverts back to Ben-Haim's original pastoral, reflective mood, and immediately negates the *espressivo molto* with the admonition, *senza espressione*. The analysis adds that the use of opening notes in a different position as well as Ben-Haim's special brand of unison writing, work together to create the composer's original mood. An ethereal sound, like a memory of what came before, is needed here.

Three Songs Without Words

Regarding the instrumental performance, the composer has said that "an instrumentalist playing the *Three Songs* should renounce all tendencies of virtuoso brilliance in favor of a purely melodic expression."
The piece may be played on virtually any instrument with piano accompaniment, or by using its orchestral version arranged by the composer.

Arioso

The analysis shows that Ben-Haim deliberately contrasted a dreamy melody marked *dolce e cantabile* against sharply dissonant repeated chords. The player must articulate these chords as evenly as possible, exactly following Ben-Haim's precise pedal marks. The melodic fragment in the accompaniment at m. 4 imitates the previous phrase in the solo part.

Players whose hands are too small to reach the tenths in m. 6 and similar places should break the chords on the beat. That is, play the bottom note of the tenth with the right-hand part and fill in the rest of the notes as quickly and quietly as possible.

Obviously, Ben-Haim felt that sustaining the D in the bass at m. 8 was important enough to sacrifice the effect of the rests by holding the pedal for the entire measure. This insures that the D will sound through.

As the analysis shows, there is a significant harmonic change at m. 22 and Ben-Haim's accent marking should be carefully observed in order to emphasize the change to C-sharp minor.

The ensuing melody in the alto part of the accompaniment must be carefully worked out so that the accompaniment chords are still are separated by the eighth-note rests.

Note that at m. 41 the opening returns in a varied form and that this time the pedal is held down through several measures even though the composer still writes in 8th rests after the dotted quarters.

Ballad

Ben-Haim marks the solo part *indifferente e quasi raccontando*, meaning "indifferently and like a story-teller."[4] In the quotation in the analysis, the composer further characterizes it as "the monotonous babbling of an Oriental story-teller." This means that both parts must be devoid of nuances so as to give that impression of the monotonous babble of an old man telling the same story for the thousandth time.

Carefully note the difference between m. 4 where Ben-Haim wants the minor second in the bass to sound through the measure against the solo's 16th notes, and m. 24 where the same 16th note pattern is in the piano part. Here the composer wants a different effect: a two-note phrase with the second note short and staccato.

All pedal markings are very exact and must be adhered to precisely as indicated.

Sephardic Melody

The improvisatory nature of this movement makes coordination between solo and accompaniment a real problem, especially in places like m. 10 where the piano's uneven run is against steady 8th notes in the solo part.

The uneven division of the runs into triplet 8ths, triplet 16ths and 32nd notes must be exactly followed. If Ben-Haim had simply wanted an upward rush he would have undoubtedly known how to write that.

Variations on a Hebrew Melody

Trio for violin, violoncello and pianoforte.

There are two kinds of performers, those who are extroverted and those who are introspective. Ben-Haim's music often reflects a pastoral character in which the performer's role is to bring the audience to the music rather than give everything away in empty showmanship. Much of his music represents an introspective personality inhabiting two different worlds—East and West.

Introduction and Theme

The tempo markings of both movements should be precisely followed and the instrumentalists should explore how to create different degrees of soft as the composer intended. However, the quiet intensity is occasionally interrupted by outbursts of *forte*. Throughout the entire piece it should be remembered that when the melody moves to a long note, for example mm. 2 and 4 of the Introductio and mm. 48, 52 and 58 of the Theme, that long note should predominate, and short notes should move to longer notes. All chords should be held for their full value, and a distinction should be made between choppy, accented notes and long, sustained trilled notes, for example the first four measures of the Introduction. Loud passages should not be played percussively, but with the deep, rich sound of determination and strength. (Mm. 9 and 15 of the Introduction).

All trills in the piano part should be pedaled. In fugal sections, the instrumentalists should listen to the end of the subject and enter as though it was a continuation of the previous statement. (Mm. 5 and 11 of the Introduction, as shown in the analysis). The rhythms should be correct, but not unyielding. Though the downbeat is often obscure, the pianist must be like a conductor and keep the first beat clear. Which ever instrument has the melody, should be dominant.

Generally long notes should be pedaled, but the pedal should not be overused. Since there are so many repetitions of short motifs, these should be played with varying dynamics, for example mm. 47-58 of the Theme. Melodic elaboration and chromaticism should be highlighted. (Mm. 47-50 of the Theme). A four-bar phrase, for example, should sound like a long line rather than measure to measure or note to note. This may be accomplished by consciously knowing beforehand where the music should "breathe." The performers should work together to create an atmosphere both ancient and modern. Note that the string players are directed to use mutes throughout the statement of the theme and first variation.

Variation I

The first variation is rhapsodic in character and utilizes the piano without strings. It begins with a reference to the material from the third measure of the theme. Melodic fragments are extended and elaborated upon, as in mm. 80-84. The counter melody in the left hand should be emphasized at its second appearance (m. 84). The long notes such as the first D sharp in the right hand of m. 81 and all others which fall on first beats must be stressed. In all cases, it must be remembered that the half notes represent the melody's goal.

The opening melody in the right hand of Variation I is taken directly from m. 49 of the Theme, and the left hand (mm. 83-84) is the Theme's second half. In this first variation, however, the melody which was originally given to the violin and cello is now distributed between the pianist's hands and is transposed to a different key.

As more flourishes occur, such as the 32nd-note runs in mm. 86, 88 and 90, the performer must maintain the indicated *piano* marking, all the while increasing intensity. In spite of the syncopation in the left hand beginning at m. 92, signaling intensified agitation, the soft dynamic level and the *tenuto* signs must be observed. The overall effect is Oriental or Middle Eastern.

Note that the theme is shortened into two-bar phrases starting at m. 95 and that the music builds to a higher dynamic level. The theme becomes thicker in texture as chords replace single notes and so the pianist's arm weight must be used. These chords must be played with the fleshier part of the fingers, rather than the fingertips, to help bring out the thickened sound quality.

Preceded by a brilliant 32nd-note run at m. 91, the texture becomes thinner and the run melts into a haunting melody. This is a diminution of the Theme's mm. 49-50. The variation fades off into a whisper.

Variation II

Unlike Variation I, which is rhapsodic and longing in mood, Variation II has a lighter, dance-like feeling and is marked *Allegretto grazioso*. As the analysis shows, it is like a scherzo, a strong contrast to the previous material. Ben-Haim's metronome marking confirms this. The strings are directed to remove mutes, (*senza sordino*), creating a more open sound.

The initial melody in the violin part is lively and perky and starts on an up-beat. The pianist's accompaniment pattern gives the music a carnival atmosphere. Each time the up-beat figuration occurs, it should be played like an up-beat and not like the end of the previous phrase. The violin's melody is repeated three times (differently each time), before finally arriving at F sharp.

The string players should use a *spiccato* bowing wherever the notes are marked *staccato* and all the performers should be aware that the initial motif in Variation II is a diminution of the Theme. At m. 130, the violin's part is a reiteration of the original Theme, and must be played legato.

The runs starting at m. 137 should be executed with cadenza bravura, but still keeping Ben-Haim's characteristic asymmetrical groupings. The piano has the more technically brilliant part starting at m. 145, which should be played with clarity and articulation culminating at m. 150 which is marked *forte*, and is the climax of the variation. The harmonics required of the string players from m. 164 suggest a nostalgic, "other worldly" quality which is a highly effective ending after the tumultuous climax.

Variation III

This variation is a march in the Stravinsky manner — dissonant and highly syncopated. The chromatic progression in the alto and bass voices of the chords and the primitive sounding open intervals at the beginning of the variation should be emphasized.

The cello part, which introduces the melody, should begin with a strong attack because the succeeding sixteenth notes grow out of the long A. These sixteenths must be executed with détaché bowing style and the piano part needs to be played with a light but firm wrist staccato.

The triplet figure at m. 176 takes on a military character and must be played with determination. At m. 178 the piano part, marked, "hard and dry" *(duro e secco)* is reminiscent of a snare drum in a marching band. In the piano part, arm weight should be used to play the thicker chords at m. 183. The piano's E-flat *sforzando* octave at m. 185 should be forcefully emphasized. Note that it implies a tritone from the preceding A octave on the first beat of m. 184, which was introduced in the second measure of the Theme. At m. 193, the soprano and tenor have a unison melody above the sextuplets which must be brought out by dropping an each accented note. The treatment of the violin melody at m. 199 is the second half of the original theme transformed into a Bedouin chant.

The variation ends with the triplet figure in the strings sounding like a fanfare and must be played with clarity and force. The brilliant ending is highlighted with a glissando on the piano.

Variation IV

The time signature of this variation, eight-four, is unusual. It shows Ben-Haim's desire for a continuous dialogue and long, uninterrupted melodic lines between the instruments. Three different phrasings must be observed at the start of this variation: namely, legato in the violin, pizzicato in the cello part and staccato in the piano.

There is a climax at m. 230 marked *forte* which all the performers need to build up to. Note that the pizzicato chord in the cello part is marked *fortissimo* indicating that the cello must produce a full sound so as to hold its own with the other instruments.

At letter K Ben-Haim reiterates a rhythmic idea, consisting of three 8th notes and a 16th note triplet which is insistent in its repetition of an almost primitive motif.

Example 33. *Trio,* Variation IV, m. 231.

This figure demands decisive articulation and clarity

There are three words to take note of in mm. 235- 236: *Morendo,* and *Quasi niente,* meaning "dying away," and "almost nothing." When executed properly, this ending is just as striking as the *fortissimo* ending of Variation III. If the music breathes properly, and is given a light and firm staccato touch, the performers will bring the audience to them, as mentioned above.

Variation V

The sixteenth-note triplet figure which ends Variation IV leads directly without a break into the next variation, which is marked, *Molto vivace e tempestoso*. Although the sound created by the three instruments is contemporary, the style is Baroque with its perpetual motion, polyphonic texture and "walking bass." Ben-Haim in fact, thought that Bach was the greatest composer that ever lived.

Because of the *staccatissimo* marking at m. 239, the piano part must be played with "sharp" fingertips, staying very close to the keys. When the music consists of long lines, as in mm. 243-250, it is necessary for the performer to perceive the musical idea in small groups and to give it a beat, so as to bring out certain important notes, although not all. One way of realizing this is to think of the last three 8th notes in m. 243 and all similar rhythms as the beginning of the next phrase.

The violinist, on the other hand, needs a heavier sound for the pizzicato octaves starting at m. 244. Beginning at m. 248 these octaves constitute an augmentation of the theme, while the melody at m. 316 is a diminution of the same theme.

The music builds to a stunning climax of orchestrally conceived bravura and trumpet-like fanfares, but even here the performers must strive for proper balance and a full sound.

Variation VI

This variation harks back to the first statement of the Theme in mood and feeling; however, it is even slower than the Theme. The oft-repeated motif:

Example 34. *Trio,* Variation VI, m. 336.

must be played with careful articulation within the *pianissimo* setting, realizing Ben-Haim's direction: *chiaro e dolce*. At the same time, he indicates the dampers should be raised for the first five measures, giving a muffled, impressionistic haze to the music. The word *simile* indicates that this pedal effect should be continued throughout the entire variation. The pianist's left hand plays an ostinato figure based on the pentatonic scale.

The cello part beginning at m. 340 should be thought of as one four-bar phrase in spite of the shifting meter and melodic fragmentation. Combined with the use of an augmented second, this gives the phrase a decidedly Middle-Eastern flavor. The following phrase in the cello part, mm. 344-347, with its use of rubato and rhythmic variation suggests the chanting of a cantor.

At m. 353 the piano has an augmented version of the flute-like motif, requiring heavier arm weight. This is followed by a much thinner sound from the strings as they are asked to play *sul tasto* which produces a more transparent sound by bowing near the finger board. At m. 356 the piano restates the theme from the Introduction for the first time, and this leads to a restatement in the strings of the Theme played in unison with mutes (m. 361) while the piano continues its ostinato figure based on the pentatonic scale.

There is a Chinese proverb which states that there is power in emptiness; as soft muted sounds can often reach deeper into the human soul that shouting can. This piece makes it points through quiet and inner tranquility rather than bombast.

Improvisation and Dance

This piece is constructed with two contrasting themes. The first is rather disjunct and dreamy, in an improvisatory style. The second theme, introduced at m. 57 with a short piano introduction, is more straightforward, dance-like and staccato in character. These two themes are in striking contrast to one another. There is also a bit of material, introduced in the violin at m. 16 which is much like a recitative.

As the analysis shows, the main climax to work toward is at m. 100 which occurs in both instruments. Before that, however, the piano part calls for an apreggiated accompaniment in the opening measures where the pedal should be used as directed for a harp-like effect. Also, at times the first bottom note may be held slightly longer in cadenza-like, improvisatory fashion. In any event, the opening indication, *Molto Rubato,* should always be kept in mind.

Ben-Haim gives detailed directions about dynamics which are mostly subdued and should be played with a quiet intensity.

He also gives the indication, *lusingando*, meaning tender, intimate. It invites the pianist to caress the keys.

A contrasting staccato touch is called for at m. 36 with a busier, repeated 32nd-note motive played with a light, loose wrist. The violin has an improvisatory opening statement played alone until m. 15. The dynamics shift between the extremes of *piano* and *forte*. Four-bar phrasing is appropriate because melodic fragments comprise much of the melody. Since there are so many meter changes, both instruments should play to the first beat and make phrase endings and beginnings very clear.

Up to m. 29, the bowing is generally legato, but at m. 29 spiccato is called for. Also the glissandi at mm. 16 and 109-110 are important because they suggest a vocal slide which is often found in Middle Eastern music.

At m. 57, the dance theme is introduced which is very light-hearted and almost sounds like a Chasidic tune. The performers should play this with a lighter touch and accent the trilled 1st beat in the violin which is what gives it the particular Chasidic character. The pianist should also bring out the syncopated rhythm in his part. It should be noted that the pedal is not carried through at m. 57. Everything should build to m. 110 as mentioned above.

Immediately at m. 111 the *martellato* marking is to be continued but at a lower dynamic leading to a transition section at m. 115 where the violinist may use more bow and attack each 2nd clearly and repeatedly. The harmonics are important to note, giving a sense of abandon to this work.

As the analysis shows, at m. 130, the dreamy and tender section marked *languidezza* returns, providing an architectural logic to this work. The short *presto con fuoco* section ending the piece requires both energy and sound from the piano and the violin.

Arabic Song

This piece is intended for solo voice (unspecified) or solo instrument (also unspecified). It is literally a song without words and, with its liberal use of augmented seconds, is highly evocative of Middle Eastern atmosphere.

The analysis shows that although the accompaniment is largely in the background, the solo part (voice or instrument) is quite passionate and culminates in its first climactic point at m. 10.

The accompaniment alternates between harp-like effects as in mm. 1-15 and percussive ones starting at m. 24 and continuing to the end of the piece. Ben-Haim uses the word *secco* alternating with pedal markings in this ending section, quite precisely indicating the effect he wants. It can be assumed that since there is no marking to the contrary, the opening should be played using the damper pedal. This is especially obvious since the composer wants the low B to sound throughout the first 8 measures.

The meter changes must be strictly observed, although a too rigid adherence to them would destroy the improvisatory quality of the piece.

The solo part must be sung or played with determination and in a cantabile style, as is indicated. Particular attention should be paid to all accents as they lend the piece its character of speech.

As pointed out the analysis, when the accompaniment returns after two measures rest, at m. 24, it is evocative of small drums, bells and cymbals. To create this effect, the pianist should pay particular attention to the *secco* marking, holding the long tied note lightly and strictly following every rest, while rolling the left hand chords quickly and decisively.

The improvisatory quality of this work calls for the two performers to listen carefully to each other, especially at solo entrances.

Notes

1. Josef Lhevinne, *Basic Principles in Pianoforte Playing*. (Philadelphia: Theo. Presser Company, 1924).
2. Paul Ben-Haim, preface to 1953 edition of "Melody and Variations." (Tel-Aviv: Israeli Music Publications, 1953).
3. Paul Ben-Haim, preface to the piano score of "Three Songs Without Words." (Tel-Aviv: Israeli Music Publications, 1952).
4. Ibid.

Chapter Thirteen

SUMMARY AND CONCLUSIONS

Ben-Haim is to be considered a composer of first rank because he created his own original style which revealed a high level of craftsmanship and artistry. He is recognized as Israel's foremost composer by leading authorities and the world's greatest artists have performed his works.

It was the intent of this researcher to inform musicians of the existence of these works and to show in them a synthesis of Eastern and Western elements.

Ten compositions by Paul Ben-Haim have been examined in this study: three for piano solo, four for piano and some other instrument(s) and three for solo instrument or ensemble without piano.

The first chapter includes a discussion of the method of analysis used as well as a review of pertinent literature. The second chapter is an overview of Israeli music and the life of Ben-Haim. Subsequent chapters are an analysis of each of the ten compositions. Chapter 12 is a performance guide for each of the 10 works which gives interpretive suggestions and is derived from data resulting from an analysis of stylistic and structural elements indigenous to each work.

After studying many of Paul Ben-Haim's works, it is evident that he is a modal-harmonic, neo-classical composer who tended toward a lyrical, pastoral, dance-like style after his immigration to Palestine in 1933. There, Ben-Haim evolved into a composer who had a deep desire to create a new musical language expressing his love for his new homeland yet not letting go of the old Germanic tradition. The result of this was a synthesis of East and West, ancient and modern, tonal and modal-harmonic. Paul Ben-

Haim's music displays a high order of technical competence and expert craftsmanship combined with an intense and wide-ranging emotional landscape. Although his formative years were spent in Germany and his musical training was in the solid German tradition of order and discipline, he found his own voice without difficulty after he reached his ancestral homeland in Israel.

Ben-Haim's music frequently reflects two worlds; exotic, mysterious oriental-sounding melodies, coupled with Western harmonies and formal designs. Pieces like his *Sonatina* display a clear dichotomy between these two seemingly opposite poles. The first movement has melodies which have a distinct Middle-Eastern flavor, with their frequent embelishments and shifting major and minor modes; however, much of the phrasing follows a regular two-bar pattern and the sonata form is very clear-cut.

Although capable of creating works in which strict formal organization is a controlling factor, some of Ben-Haim's music displays a quasi-improvisatory style, a feeling of spontaneity which is typical of the Middle Eastern-Arabic musical milieu which often inspired him.

The second movement of *Sonatina* is an example of this stylistic trait. On the other hand, his German background and training are evident in the balance, symmetry and control of form displayed in the first movement.

Harmonically, many of Ben-Haim's pieces are bi-tonal or modal and reflect the impressionistic influence of Debussy and Ravel. There is tonal ambiguity in much of his writing, a deliberate obscuring of what would otherwise be a clear-cut harmony. For example, "Pastoral" from *Five Pieces for Piano* ends with an A minor chord with an added F-sharp and D natural. The melody in the first two measures strongly suggests bi-tonality and appears to have elements of both pentatonic and whole-tone scales, but clearly ends in A minor with an added F-sharp. This tonal ambiguity prevails throughout the whole piece with a very strong feeling of A minor in the right hand and major seconds added for coloristic effect in the left. The last measure ends with a fermata on A, seeming to finally establish the elusive tonality of A, but even here the tonality is obscured by the final chord with its additional F-sharp and D.

Another example is found in "Intermezzo." The first few measures introduce an immediate clash in the harmony. The right hand points to A-flat major, while the left hand refers to E-flat minor, creating bi-tonality which is characteristic of Ben-Haim's writing. Although A-flat major seems to win out at the conclusion of the piece, there is that rumbling major second — A-flat, B-flat — in the bass in the last measure against a clear A-flat major chord. This harmony does in fact mesh completely with Ben-Haim's concept of dreaminess; it is found in every aspect of the work.

Ben-Haim's music is also characterized by a unique sound quality. The overall impression of the first movement of his *Sonatina* is subdued. It begins softly and ends dying away to a whisper on the piano's lowest note, marked *pppp*. There is only one *fortissimo* at m. 53, just before the recapitulation and this is built up to by six measures of *forte*. This represents the outstanding climax of the movement.

Judging by frequency of performances, Ben-Haim's music is now out of fashion in the USA. Much of it is also out of print and very difficult to find here. However, in Israel, interest in his music is still intense and many of his works are regularly performed by leading ensembles. There is also an annual Ben-Haim competition for young musicians who play Israeli music.

Any musician looking for stimulating solo or chamber works would do well to investigate these compositions, because they speak with an individual and unique voice and they strikingly reflect the dual world of Israel and the West.

Chapter Thirteen

Ben-Haim, was one of a number of composers who were uprooted from their native land and were forced to settle in a new country for one reason or another. Beethoven moved from Germany to Austria, Stravinsky from Russia to the USA, Bartok from Hungary to the USA. However, few of them strove to synthesize his native musical language with his new environment and culture as Ben-Haim did.

On a personal note, this researcher was introduced to Ben-Haim's music as a teenager. She had the honor and privilege of performing his *Toccata* for him during one of his visits to the USA. This remains one of her most treasured memories, especially since Ben-Haim was very complimentary about the performance. She has always felt a love and affinity for his piano works and has performed them at every opportunity.

Bibliography

Apel, Willi, ed. *Harvard Dictionary of Music*, 2nd edition, revised and enlarged. (Cambridge Mass: Harvard University Press, 1968).

Avni, Tzvni, "The Israeli Composer and His Works," Israel Music Weeks: The League of Composers in Israel. (Tel Aviv: The League of Composers, 1966).

Ben-Haim, Paul. Letter to Anita Hepner, 29 December, 1970. Anita Hepner, "The Vocal Works of Paul Ben-Haim ." Master's Thesis. (Queens College, New York, 1972).

_____.Private interview with Anita Hepner in Tel Aviv, March 1970. Hepner, p. 120.

Bernstein, Giora George, "The Influence of Oriental Musical Idioms on the Contemporary Music of Israel," unpublished dissertation for the degree of D.M.A., (Boston University, 1966).

Brod, Max. *Israel's Music*. (Tel Aviv: Sefer Press, Ltd., 1951).

Cone, Edward T. *Musical Form and Musical Performance*. (New York: W.W. Norton & Company, Inc., 1968).

Dagan, Peretz, ed. *Who's Who in Israel*. (Tel Aviv: Israel Press Ltd., 1978).

Dalhaus, Carl, Ed. Riemann *Musik Lexikon*. (Mainz, Germany: C. Dalhaus and B. Schott's Sohne, 1975).

Eisenstein, Judith Kaplan. *Heritage of Music: the Music of the Jewish People*. (New York: Union of American Hebrew Congregations, 1972).

Friskin, James and Irwin Freundlich. *Music for the Piano.* (New York: Holt Rinehart and Winston, Inc., 1954).

Gradenwitz, Peter. *The Music of Israel.* (New York: W.W. Norton & Company, Inc., 1949).

_____.*The Music of the Jews.* (New York: W.W. Norton & Company, Inc., 1956).

_____*Music and Musicians of Israel.* Jerusalem: Youth Department of the Zionist Organization, 1952.

Green, Douglass M. *Form in Tonal Music.* (New York: Holt, Rinehart and Winston, Inc., 1965).

Hindemith, Paul. *The Craft of Musical Composition.* (New York: Schott, 1942).

_____. *A Concentrated Course in Traditional Harmony.* (New York: Schott, 1944).

Hirshberg, Jehoash. *Ben-Haim, His Life and Works.* (Tel Aviv: Am Oved Publishers, 1989).

Holde, Artur. *Jews in Music.* (Tel Aviv: Bloch Publishers, 1974).

Idelsohn, Abraham Zvi. *Jewish Music in its Historical Development.* (New York: Schocken Books, 1967).

_____. *Thesaurus of Oriental Hebrew Melodies.* (Berlin: Haerz, 1914-1932).

Israeli Music Publications Ltd. "Paul Ben-Haim. A Short Biography Published on the Occasion of the Composer's 70th Birthday." (Tel Aviv: Israeli Music Publications, Ltd. 1967).

Kennedy, Michael. *The Concise Oxford Dictionary of Music*, 3rd ed, Landman, Issac, eds. (London: Oxford University Press. 1980).

La Rue, Jan. *Guidelines for Style Analysis.* (New York: W.W. Norton & Company, Inc., 1970).

Matthay, Tobias A. *Musical Interpretation.* (Freeport, NY: Books for Libraries Press, 1970).

Persichetti, Vincent. *Harmony.* (New York: W.W. Norton & Company, Inc., 1961).

Polin, Claire, C.J. *Music of the Ancient Near East.* (New York: Vantage, 1957).

Rochel, Chedva, and Jacob Gelman. Catalogue for an Exhibition in Memory of Paul Ben-Haim. (Jerusalem: Jewish National and University Library, 1985).

Rothmüeller, Aron Marko. *The Music of the Jews.* (Cranbury, NJ: A.S. Barnes Co., Inc., 1960).

Sadie, Stanley, ed., *The New Grove Dictionary of Music and Musicians.* (London: Macmillan Publishers, 1980).

Schaal, Richard, "Walter Courvoisier." *Die Musik in Geschichte und Gegenward*, part 18, 19; cols. 1752-53, (Kassel, Germany: Bärenreiter-Verlag, 1949).

Shiffers, Judith L. "An Analysis of Selected Cello Compositions by Israeli Composers: The Synthesis of East and West." Ph.D. dissertation, (New York University. 1981).

Slonimsky, Nicolas, ed. Baker's Biographical Dictionary of Musicians, 6th ed. (New York: G. Schirmer, Inc., , 1987).

Stein, Erwin, *Form and Performance*. (New York: Alfred A. Knopf, 1962).

Stein, Leo. *Structure and Style*. (New York: W.W. Norton & Company, Inc., 1970).

Toeplitz, Uri, ed. *The New Grove Dictionary of Music and Musicians*. (London: Macmillan, 1980).

The Universal Jewish Encyclopedia. (New York: The Universal Jewish Encyclopedia, Inc., 1943).

Wellesz, Egon, ed. *New Oxford History of Music: Ancient and Oriental Music*. 11 vols. (London: Oxford University Press, 1957).

Wigoder, John, ed. *Encyclopaedia Judaica*. 12 vols. (Jerusalem: Keter Publishing House, Ltd., 1971).

Zephirah, Bracha. *Kolot Rabbim (Many Voices)*; Oriental Jewish Hyms and Songs. (Tel Aviv: Massada Press, 1979).

Appendix A

List of Published Compositions by Paul Ben-Haim

Orchestral

Concerto Grosso, 1931.
Pan, Symphonic Poem, 1931.
Pastoral Variée, Solo clarinet, harp, string orchestra, 1935.
Symphony No. 1, 1940
Evocation, violin and orchestra, 1942.
Symphony No. 2, 1945.
Fanfare to Israel, band/orchestra, 1950.
"From Israel," Suite, 1951.
Three Song Without Words, 1952.
The Sweet Psalmist of Israel, 1953.
To the Chief Musician, 1958.
Violin Concerto, 1960.
Dance and Invocation, 1960.
Capriccio, piano and orchestra, 1960.
Cello Concerto, 1962.
Piano Concerto, 1963.
The Eternal Theme, 1965
Divertimento, flute and chamber orchestra, 1971-2.

Vocal

Yoram, Oratorio, 1931.
Liturgical Cantata, baritone, chorus, orchestra/organ, 1950.

Three Songs Without Words, for piano and voice, 1952
A Book of Verses, chorus, 1958.
Vision of a Prophet, Cantata, tenor and chorus, orchestra, 1959.
Lift up Your Heads, Motet, soprano and 8 Instruments, 1961.
Arabic Song, voice and piano, 1962.
Three Psalms, solo voices, chorus, orchestra, 1962.
A Hymn to the Desert, solo baritone, chorus, orchestra, 1963.
Myrtle Blossoms from Eden, soprano, piano, chamber orchestra, 1966.
Friday Evening Service, soprano, tenor, chorus, organ 9 instruments, 1967.
Six Sephardic Songs, chorus, 4 voices, 1971.

Chamber and Instrumental

String Trio, 1927.
Piano Quartet, 1931
First Suite, 1933.
Second Suite, 1935.
Nocturne, for piano, 1935.
String Quartet, 1937.
Clarinet Quintet, 1937.
Trio, for violin, cello and piano, 1939.
Sonatina, for piano, 1946.
Five Pieces for Piano, 1948.
Melody with Variations, for piano, 1950.
Sonata in G for Unaccompanied Violin, 1951
Three Songs Without Words, for piano and instrument, 1952.
Serenade, for flute and string trio, 1952.
Sonata, for piano, 1953.
Arabic Song, for solo voice or instrument and piano, 1962.
Improvisation and Dance, for violin and piano, 1971.

Appendix B

Discography

"A Star Fell Down." (Kochav Nafal) Three Poems by Matti Katz Ursula Mayer-Reinach, contralto; Paul Ben-Haim, piano. Musical Heritage Society 1654

"Arioso." from Three Songs Without Words. Albert Catell, cello; Edward Gold, piano. Musical Heritage Society 1653

"Berceuse Sfaradite." Theodore Mamlock, violin; Richard Laugs, piano. Musical Heritage Society 3186

"Capricio for Piano and Orchestra." Jerusalem Symphony Orchestra, Pnina Salzman, piano; Harth/Singer, conductor.

Concerto Grosso for String Orchestra. The MGM String Orchestra, Izler Soloman, conductor.

"Fanfare to Israel." (Truah Le'Israel). The Gadna Symphony Orchestra. S. Ronly-Riklis, conductor.

The First Symphony. Royal Philharmonic Orchestra, K. Alwyn, conductor. CBS (Israel) S72629

"Five Pieces for Piano." Amiram Rigal, piano. Music Library Recordings MLR 7077.

From Israel." The Symphony of the Air, Leopold Stokowski, conductor. United Artists UAS 8005.

"Pastorale Variée." for clarinet solo. The Louisville Orchestra, R. Whitney, conductor; James Livingston, clarinet.

"Poem" for harp. Adina Har-Oz, harp. Jerusalem Records ATD 8505

"Psalm XXIII - Adonai Ro'i." Jerusalem Symphony Orchestra, Lukas Foss, conductor; Ursula Mayer-Reinach, contralto.

"Sadot Sheba Emek." Sidor Belarsky Sings. A Salute to Israel's 20th Anniversary. Audio tape; Workmen's Circle Bookshop. 45 E. 33rd St. NYC.

"Sephardic Melody." Albert Catell, cello; Edward Gold, piano. Musical Heritage Society MHS 1653-1654.

"Serenade" for flute and string quartet. New Israel String Quartet; Aurele Nicolet, flute. RCA Victor YJRL 1-0547.

Sonata in G for Violin Solo. Yehudi Menuhin, violin. Musical Heritage Society MHS 3241.

Sonatina. Arie Vardi, piano. RCA Victor YJRL 1-0004.

Suite, Op. 34. David Bar-Ilan, piano.

"Sweet Psalmist of Israel." New York Philharmonic, Leonard Bernstein, conductor. Columbia MS 6123.

Symphony No. 2, Op. 36. Royal Philharmonic Orchestra. K. Alwyn, conductor. Stradivari SCD 8003.

Three Pieces for Cello Solo. Uzi Wissel, cello. RCA Red Seal RL83002.

"Three Songs Without Words." Arnold Sklar, viola; Joyce Sklar, piano.

"Three Songs Without Words for Cello and Piano." Michael Haran, cello; Alexander Volkov, piano. Music in Israel MII-CO-7.

"To the Chief Musician," Metamorphosis for Orchestra. The Louisville Orchestra, R. Whitney, conductor. LOU 601.

"Toccata for Piano." from Op. 34. Amiram Rigai, piano. Musical Heritage Society MHS 1653-1654.

Appendix C

Letters Reflecting Paul Ben-Haim's Stature

Mr. Paul Ben-Haim
11 Aharonowitz Street
Tel-Aviv, Israel
19 November, 1963

Dear Mr. Ben-Haim;

    Everyone in the orchestra, in our audience, and I myself, wish to thank you for the pleasure we had in playing and listening to your concerto. We found it quite difficult orchestrally, but as we had four rehearsals we were able to know the spirit of the music more deeply. Mr. Rigai played with great power and brilliance and we all wished that you might have been present.

With admiration and friendly greetings,

Sincerely,

Leopold Stokowski

Mr. Paul Ben-Haim
11 Aharonovitz Street
Tel-Aviv, Israel

November 5th, 1952

Dear Mr. Ben-Haim:

    It is with great pleasure to know that you have accepted the commission of the Koussevitsky Music Foundation. It is the Foundation's wish that the work you write be written specifically for the projected Jerusalem festival in the Spring of 1954. Since this Festival is supposed to celebrate the 5000th anniversary of King David, it is our hope that you can write a work which will relate in one way or another to the subject of King David. The work could be the setting of a Psalm or a group of Psalms, or a work relating to David as abstractly or as programatially [sic] as you wish.
    I sincerely hope that this noble idea around which the Festival will be built will inspire you to write a beautiful work. The length of the composition is up to you, but I should think it would be at least fifteen or twenty minutes long. I should be pleased if you will keep me informed of the progress of this composition, and I look forward to seeing you again in Israel.

With all good wishes.

Very Sincerely,

Leonard Bernstein

Mr Paul Ben-Haim
c/o Israeli Music Publications
PO Box 6011
Tel-Aviv, Israel

January 20th, 1969

Dear Mr Ben-Haim;

    Please accept belated thanks for your Violin Concerto that was sent to me by request of Zvi Zeitlin.

    The work is very pleasing and straightforward and met with a warm and well-deserved reception in Los Angeles.

    Compliments, greetings, and all good wishes.

Yours,

Jascha Heifetz

Index

Aeolean mode 22, 31, 49
Arabic Song 3, 199
Augsburg Opera House 14, 18

Bartok, Bela 16
Ben-Haim, Paul
  birth 13
  Christianity, conversion to 13
  creative periods 14
  East and West, synthesis of 17
  health as a child 13
  Israeli State Prize 2
  mother 13
  new name 15
  new national identity 16
  obituary 18
  perfect pitch 14
  Piano Quartet 2
  school grades 14
  String Quartet 2, 17
  teacher, as 2

Beethoven, Ludwig van 70
Bernstein, Leonard 2, 19, 250
Bizet, Georges 16
Bruckner, Anton 14

Chopin, Frédéric 52
Concerto Grosso 15
Couperin, François 18
Courvoisier, Walter 14

Davar Children's Weekly 66
Debka (Arabic dance) 12

Eastern Mediterranean School 16

Five Pieces for Piano 39
Frankenburger, Paul 13
Freundlich, Erwin 3, 21
Friskin, James 3, 21

Gorali, Moshe 67
Gradenwitz, Peter 2, 16

Harrison, Jay 15
Hebrew Arts School 19
Heifetz, Jascha 2, 251
Hindemith, Paul 18
Hora 12, 32
Huberman, Bronislaw 11

Idelsohn, Abraham Zvi 15, 18
Improvisation and Dance 192
Israel Composers' Association 15, 19
Israel Philharmonic Orchestra 11
Israeli Composer's Union 19
Israeli War of Independence 12, 18

Jerusalem Academy of Music 15
Joel Engel Prize 2

Kellerman, Berthold 14
Klose, Friederich 14

La Rue analysis 3, 4
Liszt, Franz 14, 31
Lhevinne, Josef, 214

Melody and Variations 66
Mozart, Wolfgang Amadeus 14
Müenchner Schule 14
Munich State Opera 14

National Music Council 19
Nazism 14
Neues vom Tage 18
New York Herald-Tribune 15
New York Times 18
Nietzsche, Friedrich 16

Palestine 14, 16
Palestine Philharmonic Orchestra 15
Palestine Symphony Orchestra 11
Pan (Symphonic Poem) 15
Pareles, Jon 18

Quintet for Clarinet and String Quartet 128

Ravel, Maurice 21, 39
Reinhold, Walter 4

Schalit, Heinrich 17
Schonberg, Harold C. 19
Serenade 174
Sonata in G for Violin Solo 156
Sonatina 21
State Music Teachers Training College 11
Stokowski, Leopold 2, 249
Sweet Psalmist of Israel, The 19

Three Songs Without Words 75
Tombeau de Couperin, Le 39
Toscanini, Arturo 11

Variations on a Hebrew Melody 94

Wagner, Richard 16
World War II 12

Yoel Engel Prize 2

Zephirah, Bracha 15, 18

About the Author

Pianist and performer Hadassah Guttmann was granted her Ph. D. (with honors) in music at New York University in 1991. She has been championing the music of Paul Ben-Haim since childhood and once had the privilege of performing for him. She is on the faculties of Nassau Community College, Garden City, NY and the Lucy Moses School, New York City, and was just selected as the coordinator of a new branch of the school in Far Rockaway, NY.